Perfect
weddings

one good idea can change your life...

Perfect
weddings

Make the most of your
memorable day

Lisa Helmanis

First published in 2005 by
The Infinite Ideas Company Limited
36 St Giles
Oxford OX1 3LD
United Kingdom
T: 01865 514 888
E: info@infideas.com
W: www.infideas.com

A catalogue record for this book is available from the British Library.
ISBN 1-904902-25-1

Designed and typeset by Baseline Arts Ltd, Oxford
Printed and bound by TJ International, Cornwall

Brilliant ideas

1. **Who are you?** 1
   Big fluffy meringues? A dozen under-fives dressed as fairies? Or a pint and a pork pie at
   your local? Remember, there are two of you involved so deciding what kind of wedding to
   start planning is your first big hitch in getting hitched.

2. **When: date and time** 5
   Sounds simple, but there's a lot to think about. What kind of mood do you want to set?
   Where are the guests coming from? Have you elderly relatives or small children who will be
   restless if you have a long afternoon break? And will that long break find all the groomsmen
   in the pub?

3. **The world and its mother** 9
   The issue of other people's expectations is possibly the most contentious factor in any
   wedding, and it will need nerves of steel and the good grace of Mother Teresa to keep all
   concerned happy.

4. **And so the vicar said...** 13
   Everyone is so happy that they all want to say their piece. If only you could stop them. There
   is a convention, so you need to know who does the speeches and how you handle them.

Brilliant features

Each chapter of this book is designed to provide you with an inspirational idea that you can read quickly and put into practice straight away.

Throughout you'll find four features that will help you to get right to the heart of the idea:

- *Here's an idea for you* Take it on board and give it a go – right here, right now. Get an idea of how well you're doing so far.

- *Try another idea* If this idea looks like a life-changer then there's no time to lose. *Try another idea* will point you straight to a related tip to expand and enhance the first.

- *Defining ideas* Words of wisdom from masters and mistresses of the art, plus some interesting hangers-on.

- *How did it go?* If at first you do succeed, try to hide your amazement. If, on the other hand, you don't, then this is where you'll find a Q and A that highlights common problems and how to get over them.

Introduction

Weddings count among the all-time monumental events in a person's lifetime. In any culture, they represent hope, love and the promise of a happy and fulfilling future.

And in every culture, there are also mother-in-law jokes. That's because the same joy that goes with your desire to make a commitment to one another is usually accompanied by a set of...well, let's call them challenges, shall we? And making sure that your wedding, and the run up to it, is a time that you can cherish for all the right reasons takes some careful planning, patience and a good dollop of humour.

The current fashion for grand weddings of superstar proportions (and budgets to match) means that organising them can become a full-time job in its own right. And with other aspects to balance, such as your relationship, friends, work, family and social life, it's easy to lose perspective. (And a quick note here: a great wedding is not the same as an expensive wedding, as you will see.)

So what's the secret to getting the balance right? How do you get the fantasy wedding you want and still manage to enjoy yourself? Well, the secret is in the planning and timing, and remembering why you wanted to get married in the first place. People who get married happily (as opposed to just being happily married) share the responsibilities, share the work, share the fun. And when things get tough, they keep their eye on the prize, namely that, at the end of it all, they get to be married to the person they love.

The process of planning a wedding is often also a time when you will have to cover some big issues that you haven't had to consider before, such as joint finances, family conflict and responsibility. This book will help you get the basics right, such as communication and consideration, which will be the basis for making this wedding thing work for you. On a practical level, the book will also take a look at all of the key elements for planning a wedding, and when and how to tackle them. We will take the mystery out of it for you, dividing a mammoth task into bite-size proportions.

One of the main complaints about wedding organisation relates to the pressure of the responsibility. There are many ways to deal with this. Among the key factors (which will also stand you in good stead for the rest of your life) are learning to say no and knowing when to ask for help. Handled artfully, sharing the stress can seem like bestowing honours and building bridges, improving your relationships rather than damaging them. The book even gives you chapters which will tell your nearest and dearest what to do, so you don't have to. Try simply photocopying the relevant ideas for the key wedding party members, such as the best man or speakers, and handing them over with a smile. That way it's not you making demands or suggestions; the *book* says so. Genius.

So why do the emotions surrounding a wedding get to such a fever pitch? And when should you start to regard it as a worrying sign? Well, just about everyone closely involved in the wedding will have been dreaming about this day for many years: mums imagining their daughters in wedding dresses; fathers rehearsing their speeches; sisters expecting their infant sons to be ring bearers. Many, many hopes and dreams are brought together by a wedding, and everyone will want you to grant them their little wish (usually one of many). Families are also dealing with change, something that brings up both fear and joy in equal measure. Parents can no longer pretend that you are children (even if you still get treated like one) and you will now be shifting your focus to your new partnership. So relax – panic is normal.

And when you are not panicking, you will get to enjoy all the great stuff that makes a wedding so much fun: choosing flowers; tasting cakes; trying on pretty frocks (that's mainly the girls); catching up with old friends and long lost family; and having lots of parties.

Best of all, your wedding will give you the opportunity to bring everyone you love together to watch you make a commitment to the person you intend to share the rest of life's exhilarating and bumpy journey with. It's an amazing way to start that journey off, whether you do it on a beach in the Maldives, a tiny country church or Westminster Cathedral. Good luck and congratulations.

1

Who are you?

Big fluffy meringues? A dozen under-fives dressed as fairies? Or a pint and a pork pie at your local? Remember, there are two of you involved so deciding what kind of wedding to start planning is your first big hitch in getting hitched.

This is a time when couples often try so hard to please each other that they end up pleasing no one. The best way to prevent this is individually to write down details of your dream wedding and then swap your lists. You could be very surprised.

You may think of your partner as a metropolitan sophisticate who is actually a 'hearts and flowers, 50 pageboys' traditionalist and then find otherwise. The fact is, most people (especially the female of the species) have been fantasising about this event since they were old enough to understand the fairytales that all end in 'I do'.

Here's an idea for you... **If you or your partner are visual people or find it hard to describe what you imagine in your mind, get yourself a whole stack of wedding magazines and tear out images that appeal to you. Once you have decided on the ones you both like, keep them in a file and use them as reference material for your florist, cake designer or dressmaker. It is an ideal way to make sure that you all share the same vision. After all, words can be interpreted in many different ways.**

So don't be surprised if you or your partner suddenly starts imagining glass carriages; just look at all the options before you book it – it could be your five-year-old self talking.

WHAT DO I WANT?

You will undoubtedly find that your wedding scrapbook (not a sad fanatic's obsession but an essential way to keep track of everything) seems to look like it was put together by a drunk schizophrenic. Don't be alarmed (unless you are a drunk schizophrenic) as this is often the way it goes. Instead of lamenting over the fact that you don't have one clear vision, see if there are any common denominators. Do you dither between white flowers and bright colours? Is there something connecting the pictures, like a bold use of greenery or do they all have a romantic country feel? Maybe that's the theme, rather than the specific thing you think you are looking for. Think laterally.

TOTALLY INCOMPATIBLE...

Once your list is written, if you are very lucky, you will have the same vision; more likely, you will have some similarities and some differences. Work out which are most important to you. If the bride wants several bridesmaids and the groom is a music buff, give each other an early wedding gift by handing over the decision for your favoured areas. This will also help clarify another important area, that of responsibility. Do consider consistency when sharing out responsibilities. Scrambling into a soft-top Lamborghini to head off to the reception seems more comical than romantic if the bride is sporting a vintage two-foot lace headdress.

Have a frank chat about the problems you may face ahead. Few couples make it to the big day without a few cross words, but it can be very helpful if you understand why, so take a look at IDEA 14, *How to say 'I don't' and 'you do'*.

Try another idea...

The run up to a wedding is renowned for being incredibly stressful, with one partner often feeling that they are carrying the weight of the responsibility all on their own. (No prizes for guessing which one.)

WHOSE WEDDING IS THIS?

You will almost certainly find that your wedding plans get invaded by other people's ideas. You may like the idea of running away to tie the knot on a beach but find that your family would be devastated to miss out on your big day. This is why you need to have a written 'map' of your dream wedding scenario before you announce to your nearest and dearest what your plans are. You can then refer back to it every time you feel that you are losing your way or feel bullied.

'A great marriage is not when the "perfect couple" comes together. It is when an imperfect couple learns to enjoy their differences.'
DAVE MEURER, *author*

Defining idea...

How did
it go?

Q **My future mother-in-law is taking over our wedding and we have only just got engaged. My partner always acquiesces as she is quite a formidable woman, but I don't want to march down the aisle to her tune. How do I keep her under control?**

A *Attack is, as they say, the best defence. She has probably been looking forward to this for years, so asking her to simply 'butt out' is not going to make for a happy time. Try being proactive and giving her a list of tasks to do, none of which involve decision making. Ask her to get several quotes for harpists, locating companies that can find you a white Mercedes or gathering addresses for the invites. All of these tasks are genuinely useful so she won't feel maligned or marginalised, but will also realise the decisions aren't hers to make.*

Q **What if she keeps pushing?**

A *Keep it simple and be brave. Make sure you thank her for all her efforts and suggestions, but make it clear that you don't want to burden her with such a big job. If she still doesn't get the hint, say a polite, warm 'no' and then stay quiet. Don't explain yourself, as that would suggest she has a valid argument that you must convince her against, leaving the power balance with her. Just repeat the 'no' if she persists; if she can't respect your boundaries you will have to set them more firmly, or this problem will occur through your future relationship.*

2

When: date and time

Sounds simple, but there's a lot to think about. What kind of mood do you want to set? Where are the guests coming from? Have you elderly relatives or small children who will be restless if you have a long afternoon break? And will that long break find all the groomsmen in the pub?

Choose your date carefully. If you want a big wedding, you need to be realistic about the amount of time you allow. And there are a few religious rites to consider too...

Ah, a summer wedding, it seems like the obvious choice. But it's worth thinking about the other options too. Autumnal weddings can be very romantic and lend the pictures the rich reddish hues of the season. Winter weddings add drama, which can be even more magical with an evening ceremony. Summer weddings also fall at the same time as many people's holidays, and can be really hot if you want the full ball gown silhouette wedding attire. If you have a summer wedding date in mind that has some special significance, be prepared to have to wait up to a year or two to get your perfect slot. Incidentally, June, the most popular month for weddings, is meant to be the luckiest for lovers, as it was named for the Roman God Juno, the god of love.

Is there going to be a break between the ceremony and the evening reception? You must think how your guests will spend that time. If you have grandparents, elderly or pregnant relatives or friends, then consider booking them a room in a local hotel to rest. If not, ask your reception venue if there is a restaurant or lounge area for them to relax in. Also consider that they might need some light refreshments; you mustn't leave them to fend for themselves, especially if they are in an area they don't know. If you do, you might find people retire to the nearest alehouse, and retire early from your evening a little worse for wear.

CHOOSING YOUR TIME OF DAY

Think first about the mood you want to set. Different times of day create definite moods. Outdoor evening weddings can be great in a hot summer and you can have the benefit of a pink sunset if you're lucky. A winter wedding can be given extra drama by being held at night, with great torches of fire lighting the guests' way. A spring wedding, with pretty pastel colours, can be enhanced by a morning stroll to the local church. A noon wedding can be uncomfortable if held in the midday sun, so think about the practical side as well as the romance.

RELIGIOUS TRADITIONS

Your religion may have traditions. Protestant weddings are often held in the afternoon yet Roman Catholic weddings traditionally begin at 11 a.m. or noon. If you want a Saturday wedding and you are Jewish, it will have to begin after sundown, which marks the end of the Sabbath. And you need to make sure that there are no religious holidays that will influence your choice.

AND LESS ROMANTIC...

There are slightly less interesting yet no less essential factors that need to be considered. Are you holding your ceremony in the same location as your reception? If so, you will need to ensure that the rooms will be ready immediately to move straight to the reception area. Check if there will be other weddings at the same venue on that day. Make sure there will be enough time to assemble your wedding party without confusing the guests; you don't want them ending up in the wrong room of the town hall watching another bride wander down the aisle. Also make sure that there is enough time before the service for the florists and photographer to set up. Don't be scared to ask your registry office or church how long they allow each party.

You may have to be prepared for the disappointment of finding your dream time slot unavailable, as many weddings are booked so far ahead. If that's the case, you can choose a date further in the future or accept disappointment gracefully; there is very little you can do and if you take everything to heart, you will have a rocky road ahead.

Where are the guests coming from? If many of them are coming from a long distance make sure you investigate hotels for them nearby so that they can make it to the ceremony on time.

Before you think about your time of day, consider whether or not it suits your location; see IDEA 17, *Where: choosing a location*, to make sure they work together to best effect.

Try another idea...

'We have so much time and so little to do. Strike it. Reverse it.'
ROALD DAHL, *Charlie and the Chocolate Factory*

Defining idea...

7

AVOID THE DREADED WEDDING LULL

There is often a natural lull when a band or DJ arrives and begins to transform the venue into a suitably festive reception area. The sight of someone humping around huge boxes and crawling around the floor looking for power points can often dampen the mood. To create a smoother flow from day to night, find out from your venue if the equipment can be set up before the reception begins. If this is not possible, perhaps there is another room that guests can retire to whilst tables are cleared and the party gets started.

How did it go?

Q   I want an evening banquet for my wedding, but my local registrar won't work past a certain time. Can I request that they work later?

A   *No, they are under no obligation, and you need to make sure you book well in advance to get the slot you like.*

Q   Are there any other options?

A   *Your best solution is to have a quiet official ceremony before the wedding, with close family as witnesses and then have a blessing ceremony when you want it.*

Q   So, can I do the ceremony again?

A   *Of course. That way you can fit it into your plans, and even have some fun writing your own vows.*

3

The world and its mother

The issue of other people's expectations is possibly the most contentious factor in any wedding, and it will need nerves of steel and the good grace of Mother Teresa to keep all concerned happy.

Everyone involved, from your granny to your other half's mum, will have their own list of 'must invite' cast in concrete, and don't be surprised if half of them you've never even heard of.

The best way to deal with this situation is to take control from day one. Ask all the relevant parties to write a list of their proposed guests, in order of importance. Make it clear that space and budget may mean that not everyone on their list will make it onto the final version. You and your spouse-to-be should also make separate lists, and do it as soon as you get engaged so that by the time you come to send out the invites, you've thought of everyone (rather than finding a great uncle and his brood, all the way from New Zealand, being sprung on you at the last moment, blowing both your table plan and your budget).

Here's an idea for you...

Draw up a map showing how to get to the ceremony and/or reception. These are becoming frequent inserts in wedding invitations, especially as wedding venues become more remote and elaborate. And it is a considerate touch that simplifies your guests' lives and saves a few marriages in the process. (Don't forget, couples trapped in cars lost on back roads don't make happy wedding guests.) Include both written and visual instructions, and account for the fact that guests may be coming from different directions. If you don't want to include it with your invitations, you could include a map reference for a web site. If you are choosing somewhere remote, you may need to design your own map, and tying balloons at relevant points will help to ensure that guests don't miss their turnings. Remember to include a reception card for ceremony guests if it is to be held at a different site than the service.

Order your invitations at least four months before the wedding, and allow an additional month for engraved invitations (instead of handwritten or printed).
The bride's parents traditionally issue invitations, but if the groom's parents are assuming some of the wedding expenses, the invitations should be in their names also.

Don't skimp when ordering; you will need at least twenty-five extra invites for last-minute invitees and the few you might smudge. It might seem wasteful, but you will spend a lot more if you have to reorder. Start addressing and planning at least two weeks before you want to put them in the post box; you will be amazed at how long it takes to collect all the addresses and mail the invitations. It'll be even longer if you're using a calligrapher or if your guest list is very large. A typical refusal rate runs at around 15–20%, so you might want to send out invites later to those people who had to be left out due to numbers. Make sure you can accommodate everyone: a standing-room-only policy might make you look popular, but you won't *be* popular. Also, take one invite to get weighed to make sure you have the right postage, and ask for pretty seasonal stamps if they have them.

MAKING THE NUMBERS ADD UP

A vital part of the invite process, and a boost for your sanity, is the response cards. These should be enclosed with the invitation and will help you determine the number of people who will be attending your wedding. The cards should be easy for your guests to understand and use, and make it really clear you want them returned. If necessary for working out the catering, it is acceptable to put a date on them by which guests must reply: a month before the wedding is acceptable. If you want to get a reply include a self-addressed and stamped return envelope to make it excuse-free for those bachelor friends who can't seem to master the art of buying a stamp. If it is being held in a different place, a separate card with the date, time and location for the reception should be enclosed with the ceremony invitation.

Napkins, matches and order of service may also be ordered from your stationer. See IDEA 36, *Choosing a theme for decoration*, on choosing a theme that will link them all, to create an elegant, cohesive look.

Try another idea...

WHAT TO SAY?

Invitation wording can be tricky, but luckily there are lots of conventions and systems you can stick to; or break. Your preferred stationer will have examples for you to follow.

'For 'tis always fair weather when good fellows get together with a stein on the table and good song ringing clear.'
RICHARD HOVEY, from *Spring*

Defining idea...

How did it go?

Q I don't want children squawking through the wedding, but my fiancée has told her niece she can come. What can I do?

A *The presence of children is often a big issue. Determine as early as possible if you wish to include children in the wedding party. Make it a rule and insist you both stick to it. You must be a man of steel.*

Q So I have to look like the bad guy to her niece?

A *It's all about the way you present it. You are being fair to all the children and parents, not trying to hurt just one. If you give in to one couple with their little precious, your walk down the aisle will met by a sea of glowers from other parents who had to leave their kids at home.*

Q And what can I do to stop her niece being very disappointed?

A *You may have to get around it by giving her an official role, such as a flower girl. That way you have a legitimate excuse for her inclusion.*

4

And so the vicar said...

Everyone is so happy that they all want to say their piece. If only you could stop them. There is a convention, so you need to know who does the speeches and how you handle them.

Everyone looks forward to the speeches — as long as they aren't too long. Make sure everyone tries a run through and times themselves. If any of your speakers fancies himself as a bit of a performer, make your instructions very clear: this is a toast to the happy couple, not a chance to fulfil those dreams of being on the stage.

Officially, the speeches run in the following order: the bride's father's speech, the bridegroom's speech and lastly the best man's speech. Kick off the toasts with an announcement by the toastmaster or best man, who should ask for the bride's

Here's an idea for you... **Think about changing the rules. If the bride decides that she would like to say something, or would like her maid of honour to speak on her behalf, that's all good.**

father to deliver a speech of 'health and happiness to the bride and bridegroom'. He would normally welcome the groom's parents, relatives of both families any other guests and welcome the groom to his family and say a few words about his daughter.

The bridegroom replies on behalf of himself and his bride, taking the opportunity to thank his parents and talk about his love for his bride, and thank all those present for their attendance and gifts. He will finish by toasting the bridesmaids (no, not *that* kind of toasting) and may also present them with a small gift as a token of the couple's appreciation. Next is the most awaited speech of all. It is the best man's duty to respond to the toast on behalf of the bridesmaids, and then deliver what has historically become a fun speech to warm everybody up ready for the good old knees up they should be having to give the couple a good start. And, of course, it should include a good dose of humiliation for the groom.

AND THEN I SHAVED OFF HIS EYEBROWS...

So, does the best man's feel like the most pressured speech of the day? There are tips you can give him (that might work for you, too). Firstly, relax. This is not open-mike night at your local. This audience will be rooting for you; they really want to laugh, and will even be tuned into funny bits you weren't overly impressed with yourself. Unless it's a shotgun wedding, the guests want everything to have the feel-good factor.

When faced with a blank sheet of paper, it's a good start to jot down anything that comes into your head. For the best man, writing down some facts gives an effective skeleton: how he knows the groom, when you met and how he met your partner, etc. Anecdotes about how the couple's relationship has blossomed will be well received. It is appropriate to tell stories that recall the groom's crazy, bachelor antics, but it's not the time to announce that he has slept with most of the bridesmaids. The best man will be expected to be a little risqué but not to give grandmothers heart attacks.

Can you hear me at the back? Don't mumble through it only to discover that only the top table heard you. IDEA 6, *Getting readings right*, will show you how to get professional.

Try another idea...

It may seem that every best man's speech that brought the house down was ad libbed all the way through. No such thing: always remember that no professional comedian goes on stage without any preparation so neither should any of you. Get a willing friend to listen to the speech and then consider their opinions as openly as possible. Don't get defensive if they are only trying to help.

Suggest the best man assesses his voice. If he talks in a flat, monotonous sounding way, he could practise filling it with inflection. It's surprising to discover what sounds artificial to you seems perfectly normal to others. It will also help with nerves if he feels he's playing a part rather than standing up in front of complete strangers for a rather long one-way chat. And as a general rule for all of you, slow down: most people tend to rabbit through things. If you can bear it, film yourselves with a camcorder to see which of these crimes you commit so you can rectify them as you practise.

'Always do your best. What you plant now, you will harvest later.'
OG MANDINO, US novelist

Defining idea...

15

Q **My father only has sons and is a great public speaker, and I just know he'd love the chance to do a 'father of the bride speech'. Can we cheat and do a 'father of the groom' speech too?**

A *You can do whatever you want. Just make sure that the other speeches are short enough to accommodate an extra one. There is nothing worse than the speeches starting to resemble a Japanese endurance test.*

Q **So how long is too long and how many speakers are too many?**

A *As it's your big day, you probably feel as if you could listen to your loved ones wax lyrical about your good selves all day. But consider the last wedding you went to – were the speeches so long that your eyes were rolling back in your head or did they bounce along happily with lots of laughter? Based on your experience as a guest, aim for a timing that falls into the latter category. If you have concerns, get your speakers to time themselves, then add it up (you'll be surprised how quickly it mounts up). If you can see it's going to be too much of a long haul, ask them all to shave off a minute or two.*

5

The blushing bride

But are the blushes for the right reasons? Yes, you've dreamed about this day since you were a little girl, but remember you had the figure of a twelve year old back then. It's a must to be realistic when searching for the right dress.

Always wanted to shimmer in silk but know going bra free is out of the question? Tried on a full skirt and looked like the Christmas fairy (tree included)? The trick is to choose a dress that you like, but a dress that suits you as well.

Firstly, you must not go into a bridal shop with any fixed ideas; that way madness lies. All kinds of married women will tell you that the dress they tried on for a laugh, the dress they would never have considered in a million years, turned out to be the one they tripped up the aisle in. So leave trawling the wedding magazines until you have had at least one major trying-on session.

Here's an idea for you...

When choosing your dress, think first about your hairstyle and headdress, or absence of one. Different necklines will work better with hair up or down, with veil or without, so consider these ideas. Tiaras are a popular choice and suit any length of hair, although you may need styling products and pins to help them stay put. If you want a headdress with a minimum of fuss, a simple silk Alice band or headband can be cute and '50s retro while also allowing for a windy day (Highland weddings take note). Coronets look wonderful with a long veil, and fresh flowers bring simple charm to any dress; a single exotic bloom can add real glamour. Hats need a more formal outfit, but can look dynamite with a chic trouser or skirt suit. Just bear in mind you might want to take it off later, and you'll need a hairdo that can handle it.

Your wedding dress is unlike any dress you will ever have worn. For starters, it is likely to be white or cream, and much longer, and a much more unusual shape, than anything currently hanging in your wardrobe. So throw away your preconceptions of what will suit you: you'll be wrong. Try on every shape you can get your hands on, even if you don't like the style. You are guaranteed to be surprised by what flatters you. And that goes for your complexion, too: pure white doesn't work for everyone so make sure you see the dress against your skin in daylight as well as in the shop, because your guests will.

When you have found a style that suits, compare the cost of materials. (A plain silk shift is likely to differ from a boned, beaded bodice with full skirt.) This will give you an idea of what you need to consider when setting your budget. Now you can look at the wedding magazines, to help you find variations on your theme. Bear in mind, you will need to order at least three to four months before your big day and, if you are indecisive, work back from this date to make sure you don't end up panic buying.

ANYONE COVERING YOUR BACK?

You need a dress buddy to talk you out of any childish Cinderella fantasy and give her free rein to say, 'Yes, your bum does look big in that'. (When you say your vows, most guests won't be looking at your face.) And make sure one of you remembers to bring some heels, unless you will be wearing flat (or no) shoes. Having your dress cut a few inches too short could be devastating, sartorially speaking.

Think about whether you want a theme to your wedding (colour, period, style), as this will make your choice of dress easier. See IDEA 36, *Choosing a theme for decoration.*

Try another idea...

SOME NOT-SO-EXCITING PRACTICAL CONSIDERATIONS

A lace shift in December? Nice idea; miserable wedding. Think about the season of your wedding. In high summer, cool silk, chiffon, pure cotton or lace; cooler winter months call for heavier fabrics such as brocade, velvet and duchess satin. And be practical: hiking a huge skirt through fields to a marquee might seem funny at first but will soon lose its humorous appeal.

Be positive. Write a list of all your best assets and those which you would like to show off to full advantage on the day. (Not all of them will be suitable for showing off.) A lovely off-the-shoulder number is ideal for a high neck, and a pear shape can be hidden with a slinky waist, flaunting a full skirt and nipped-in bodice. You will never have a chance to hide your disliked bits so skilfully again! And don't forget that budgets often get stretched by essentials such as underwear, stockings, shoes, jewellery, bags, scarves, etc. All will add finishing touches and complete your look, but will they bust your budget?

'I...chose my wife, as she did her wedding gown, not for a fine glossy surface but such qualities as would wear well.'
OLIVER GOLDSMITH, *The Vicar of Wakefield.*

Defining idea...

19

How did it go?

Q **The wedding is off. I've found my dream dress and *he* says no, it's too expensive for a one-off. What can I do?**

A *Ah, men and frocks. There are ways of reining in the costs whilst letting your dreams run free; consider man-made fabrics instead of silk. If you want to feel the real McCoy of silk on your skin, consider hiring your dress. Before you shriek in horror, you can pay about the same to hire a designer dress as you would to buy a mass-produced one. If you must have it, you could recoup some of the cost of a designer dress by selling it after the wedding. Lots of agencies and web sites offer this service (unless you've covered it in red wine). And how often will you wear it anyway?*

Q **No, I can't bear to part with my dress. What should I do now?**

A *Then something might have to give. Offer to compromise on another area of the wedding and tell him the dress will be a family heirloom. Preserve your dress by having it expertly cleaned and boxed, ready for your offspring's big day. Or cut it short and dye it red, and take him dancing...*

6

Getting readings right

Readings can be a wonderful way to express what's in your heart without having to emotionally put yourself on the line (especially if you are a blubberer). And the best thing is, someone has already done the work for you.

Choosing the right readings is essential because they set the tone for the whole ceremony. So, don't be too hasty in making your decision — it could help you say a great deal in a very short time.

Timing is a key factor. Make sure your readings are concise, but long enough to express your personal sentiments fully. They must not be so long that guests zone out and start reading the prayer book for relief. At the same time, anything too short will sound like a limerick, and those should be saved for the best man's speech. Get a friend to time them as you read them out – you might be surprised how quickly three stanzas can seem like a stroll through eternity.

Here's an idea for you...

Think about where and when the reading will take place. If you want to do it during the ceremony, rather than have the reader step into the place vacated by the clergyman, try having her stood slightly to the side. If the reading is long, you can break it up into sections relevant to the running of the ceremony. There are no rules here; you can even move the reading to the reception to keep the ceremony shorter, and you can drop the reading altogether if you don't feel that it works for you. And consider putting a copy of it in with guests' favours as a sweet keepsake.

WHERE TO LOOK

There are plenty of books out there dedicated to wedding readings, but spread your search wider. Is there a favourite poem or book from your childhood that has special memories? You don't have to stick with Kahlil Gibran's *The Prophet* or Shakespeare to have a meaningful reading. And think hard about what you are trying to communicate: are you trying to express your feelings for each other through the reading? If so, why not consider choosing a reading each, to be read as responses. Lots of couples choose readings that express their feelings about their relationship or what they think marriage should be about.

Readings are a lovely way of communicating your intentions towards each other and how you hope to relate to one another in the future. This is not to say you should go as far as including the lines such as 'And I will take control of the laundry basket as long as the dishwasher gets stacked straight after dinner'.

However, a light touch can be just as poignant as a seventeenth-century romantic poet. Make sure that you understand each other's tastes. Get your partner to choose three poems they like, and you do the same, and see which are the most similar in tone. You could even consider writing a reading yourself – try a witty list of intentions, or a love letter you have kept (just make sure it's one from the person you're about to walk down the aisle with).

Looking to include everyone? Check out IDEA 26, *The supporting cast*, when you are considering your reader.

Try another idea…

CHOOSING YOUR READER

Just because Aunt Maude was in amateur dramatics, it's not a good reason to let her step up to the mike. Similarly, as much as you love your gran, if she can't read your chosen passage without 2 ft cue cards, you may have to think again. You need to consider how comfortable your reader will be. Don't strong-arm a reluctant friend into participating or you will get the reading you deserve – mumbled and raced through. Choose someone who will relish the task and put some thought into its delivery; many an exquisite Shakespeare sonnet has been murdered by a lack of intonation and inflection.

'I wish thee as much pleasure in the reading as I had in the writing.'
FRANCES QUARLES, English religious poet

Defining idea…

How did it go?

Q   I love a poem that my partner hates. How can I get him to agree to what I want?

A   *It's the 'c' word that keeps coming up again and again: compromise. You need to ask yourself why you would want a reading he will be tutting through, rather than something that represents how you both feel. You will have to resume your search. Watching him smile at you lovingly during the reading, rather than seething, will be worth it. Ask him to get involved in the search so that you get a better idea of what he likes more quickly. (He might even let you have your way if that seems like too much effort.)*

Q   And he really wants his sister to do the reading. I think she has a speaking voice like a distant hover mower. She has no intonation and will send everyone to sleep. What can I do about that?

A   *This is where being benign bears fruit: after all, if you are willing to give in on your reading, it's his turn to be reasonable. If it is truly important to him, gently remind him of his sister's flat, dull tone and suggest, for everyone's comfort, she has a couple of classes in public speaking. It's something most people could benefit from (few of us get up in front of a room to deliver speeches on a daily basis). If that's too controversial, suggest all of the wedding speakers get together to practise and let the others help her (and point out her weak points).*

Q   So I might not get my way?

A   *It's not my way anymore, it's our way.*

7

Ring the changes

Tradition has it that you are supposed to hand over two months' salary for an engagement ring, and spend whatever you want on the wedding rings, which are usually cheaper because they are usually more simple. It's a big outlay so be sure you make the right choices.

You need to get to grips with some jewellery facts to make sure that you get the best sparkler for the light of your life. So how do you know what to look for?

The cut is the most essential element of the 'sparkle' and there are many of them. There are also fashionable cuts (such as a baguette cut), so you need to get yourself acquainted with them by spending a few afternoons flicking through bridal magazines and visiting a decent jeweller's. You don't want to present her with something a dowager would have loved, but she is already planning to lose.

The cut refers to the number, placement, and shape of the 'facets' (flat, polished planes) that create a finished diamond. The shape into which the stone is cut determines its brilliance (white light reflection or sparkle), and fire (reflection of

Here's an idea for you...

Think of messages you could have engraved on the inside of your rings – perhaps a pet name, the date you met, the date of your marriage or both of your initials.

rainbow colours). A good cut can release a stone's beauty, just as a bad one makes a stone dull. The next aspect to consider is the clarity, which is how clear the diamond is. The imperfections on the outside are called blemishes and the ones inside are called inclusions. This may seem like a horrifying prospect, buying a less than flawless diamond for your beloved, but most diamonds have imperfections. Another thing that may surprise you is that they are not always white, even if you might think they are. The majority are white or yellow, though they come in most colours of the rainbow. Yellow diamonds tend to be cheaper, although they don't reflect light as well. The weight of your diamond is measured in carats, which is equivalent to 200 milligrams.

So, now you know what you need to spend money on, you need to think about the style of setting. Once again, now is not the time to think about what your mum has worn. Do a bit of James Bond style spying on her. What colours does she like? Rifle through her jewellery box; does she have mainly gold or silver? If it's a mix, were some presents that she doesn't ever seem to wear? Is she an ostentatious character or does she loathe fuss? You may want to buy her a rock that has her arm dragging along the floor as a sign of your adoration, but she might feel much more appreciated and understood if you get her a simple vintage setting that reflects her style.

There are many settings to choose from, and all of them can bring something different to the stone. If you want it to really sparkle, choose something that allows as much light through the stone as possible. Traditionally, you would choose to set the stone/stones in one of the three most popular precious metals. These are gold (which comes in various shades; the silver appearance of some rings often being white gold), platinum and titanium. There are the same choices for wedding rings. When it comes to paying for these, it is traditional for the bride to pay for her husband's wedding band, and for him to purchase hers.

Do you know what your bride has in mind? If you are at a loss, get talking: look to IDEA 1, *Who are you?*, for ways to work it out.

Try another idea...

MAKING IT SPECIAL

Commissioning your own design can bring an extra special slant to your union, and will be a gesture greatly appreciated by your beloved. Although it might seem like an expensive and time-consuming approach, it could end up giving you the best value. Unmounted diamonds are by far the best deal, and you could get a setting copied if you really like it. Plus, buying a diamond already mounted means that you cannot check its quality. However, it can take weeks to get your ring made up, or to settle on a design if you are commissioning a designer, so build that into your proposal or wedding day schedules.

HOW MUCH?!!

Determine your budget and then play with the different components to get the best combination for you. Is size king or a band of smaller, well cut super sparkly gleamers that you can see from three streets away? Decide what shape, carat weight, and colour you want. And be prepared to haggle; there is often a margin for play built into the price. Then get it home, and please insure any rings before you give them to the best man.

'With this ring, I thee wed, with my body I thee worship and with all my worldly goods I thee endow.'
Wedding vow, *Book of Common Prayer*

Defining idea...

29

How did it go?

Q   **In her will, my grandmother left me her engagement ring to present to my future wife. We were close, and I would love to do that, but it's a rather old-fashioned cluster in a gold setting; my bride is a modern blonde who only wears silver. What should I do?**

A   *Lucky you. This is easy to fix. You can have the stones removed and reset. Depending on your taste, you could take the larger central stone and have it set in a silver band, and then take smaller jewels and have them turned into earrings for your wedding to her.*

Q   **Isn't it disrespectful to break up the old ring?**

A   *I'm sure your grandmother would rather the jewels were worn in some form than not at all. Why not take a photograph of it and write the lineage of it on the back as a keepsake, and your wife might choose to bequeath it to one of your kids – a family tradition could be born, but one that keeps up with the times.*

8

How to be the best best man

So, what's this best man lark all about? There is more to it than ensuring the groom is never left with an empty glass at his stag do. Traditionally, it was the best man's duty to protect the groom from bad luck, and ensure that once he had begun his journey to the church he actually got there (no matter how substantial the bribe).

Sorry, but if anything goes wrong, it kind of is the best man's fault. So here is a simple guide to what you should be doing to prove your mettle.

You should start by getting the contact details of the maid of honour or chief bridesmaid. This way you'll be able to liaise on arrangements and queries (such as "Where is the bride?!"). And although the jokes about the best man having first crack at the bridesmaids might be funny, they are just that: jokes. Those posh dresses they are wearing are not wrapping paper, and you will have to talk to them a lot in the run up to the wedding, so leave any indiscretions until the reception (where you can make a hasty retreat).

Here's an idea for you...

Offer to look after the distribution of corsages, which are part of the groom's responsibility. You should also be willing to help him choose his suit, shirt and tie. If he is the superstitious type, or if you are, arrange for the groom to carry a small mascot or charm in his pocket on the wedding day for good luck. And remove any ladders from the nearby area.

You also need to sit and work a few things out with the groom. He may ask you to help to choose the ushers and explain their duties to them, and even oversee them on the day. Compile a list of close family members who should have special seating arrangements at the ceremony and pass it on to the ushers. Transport is part of your domain too, so visit the ceremony and the reception venues to check on timings and parking arrangements; you don't want to discover the bride's limo can only stop to let her out two blocks away. (For extra points, check the traffic conditions on the big day.) You will also be expected to attend the wedding rehearsal and arrange the going-away car for the bride and groom from the reception if required. (Stick an emergency list of taxi companies on your schedule list so you can save the day should needs must.)

The day before, you are your groom's wing man, but you really need to be available to him for the whole week before and do things such as collect any hired clothing and accessories. You'll have to badger the groom to make sure he has all the necessary documents for the ceremony and the honeymoon. You also need to organise decorations for the going-away car, which can be as simple as a single ribbon, tastefully tied, or something more along the jovial theme of tin cans and shaving foam. Just make sure that the driver can still see where he's going.

Some best men also organise decoration for the honeymoon suite, especially if it is in the same location as the reception. Remember, the adult, sensitive approach to this tends to involve a bottle of chilled champagne and some soft lighting, not putting water-filled condoms in the bed. (Anything has to be an improvement on the best man who filled the couple's Jacuzzi full of washing up liquid, and then filled it full of ushers (still in hired morning suits), and filled *them* with the contents of the mini bar. The not so happy couple came in to find them all fast asleep buried in foam.)

The stag do used to be the groom's problem, but it has begun to be the best man's headache instead. This means more work, but also more opportunities for devilment. (Bear in mind, though, that no one will love or thank you for a wedding picture missing a groom. Or his eyebrows.) Try IDEA 47, *Tied to a lamp-post in Germany*, for some guidance.

Try another idea...

During the ceremony you carry and present the rings to the groom, and follow the wedding procession down the aisle after the last bridesmaid, and keep following them until you hit the reception. There you will be part of the receiving line and greet the guests. You might also be expected to carry cash to pay the band or DJ, and it is traditional for you to pay the church minister's fee, adding an odd sum to bring luck to the couple.

The next day, collect and return any hired clothing and accessories. And the chief bridesmaid.

"Friendship is mutual blackmail elevated to the level of love."
ROBIN MORGAN, US writer

Defining idea...

Q **I really want my brother to be my best man but he is notoriously lazy. I know he would be offended if I asked someone else but I don't want to end up having to organise everything for him. What can I do?**

A *Hand him this book. If he is too lazy to read it, you may need to print out a laminate for him showing a list of required responsibilities. If he won't even engage with that, maybe you need to rethink. Try telling him that you want him to have the role, but if he won't take it all on, the responsibility as well as the privilege, then you may have to ask someone else.*

Q **If I've asked my brother to be best man, and he's accepted, but I can see that he's shirking, what should I do then?**

A *If you must have him in the role, name someone as head usher and ask him for help in explaining your situation and getting the best out of your brother. Remember to make sure the third party gets suitable appreciation – a yacht might do – for his thankless behind-the-scenes toil.*

9

Ladies in waiting

Once you've charted the shark-infested waters of choosing your bridesmaids, the real work begins. You need to get them looking great, feeling great, and even being great to each other.

The bridesmaids play a pivotal role. As well as looking great (but not too great), they should be offering help, support and planning, and giving the single you a decently decadent send off. But, of course, there is one essential area that will influence how happy all of you are: the bridesmaids' dresses. Friendships have floundered over pink shantung silk and puff sleeves.

There are several variations to consider. Firstly, unless you are a member of the jet set with only models for attendants, all of yours will be different sizes, and ages. Start by asking everyone what they feel comfortable with: adult bridesmaids often feel a bit self-conscious in a full-length outfit and might prefer knee length. Empire

Here's an idea for you...

Get swatches from your dressmaker or shop, one for each bridesmaid (and a couple over in case they lose them) so each can have one to use when looking for shoes and make up.

line is great for tummy hiding, and those endowed with larger breasts might not be comfortable with spaghetti straps that rule out the support of a bra. Rather than drive yourself insane, why not choose a colour and fabric and ask them to choose variations on that theme? That way you can ensure the fighting is kept to a minimum. (And remember when choosing your fabric that flowing, clingy satin shows no mercy.) If colour matching is a problem, choose a dress style and let them pick colours from a complementary range, or different tones of one shade. Try two in one shade and two in another. But when planning your colour theme, do consider that not everyone can pull off canary yellow.

IT'S YOUR DAY, SO IT'S YOUR WAY

Don't let yourself be bullied by your bridesmaids when it comes to outfits. All women know how it feels to dislike the way you look, so it's easy to give in to their demands. But do not let them pull you in several directions. The best way to do this is to allow them their individuality by letting them choose their own shoes, bags and jewellery. You can even make their posies a little different from each other, or if one would rather not carry a posy, have a corsage in the same flowers. This way they will still feel like themselves on the day. And don't be forced away from your original idea. You don't want people looking at the wedding photographs and wondering if the bride in the Edwardian lace dress had borrowed the funky, super-modern bridesmaids from someone else's wedding just for the pictures.

HITTING STICKY ISSUES

Appointing a maid of honour might seem like unnecessary favouritism, but it is a good way of making sure that someone is keeping tabs on your lovely handmaidens other than just you. Ask her to collect the bridesmaids' measurements and to ensure that everyone has suitable underwear – your dizzy college friend wearing a black bra under her pale pink dress because she hadn't thought things through may be endearing, but will ruin the photographs. The maid of honour can also intercede if there are any disputes.

Make sure the bridesmaids are involved from the beginning so that they can raise concerns early on. Also ask them to be realistic: you need exact measurements, and do not let them claim they will lose that extra half stone only to find yourself surrounded by acres of straining seams. Bear in mind bridesmaids' dresses can take up to six months to arrive if they are being ordered from abroad.

A problem can often arise over who pays for the dresses. It is not uncommon for the bridesmaids to buy their own dresses, but think that through. Don't ask them to splash out on outfits they couldn't wear again, except to fancy dress, and don't choose something ridiculously pricey. If they can choose something they can wear again they may be happier to cough up. You need to weigh up everyone's present financial situation before settling on a style, and you may have to help out your cousin struggling through college with a donation.

Got a bridesmaid who has bird's nest hair and puts eye make up on like a five year old? Get her to read through IDEA 18, *Crowning glory*, with you to help her sharpen up her act.

Try another idea...

'Love is blind, friendship closes its eyes.'
FRIEDRICH NIETZSCHE

Defining idea...

37

HAIRSTYLE

You may consider using artificial flowers for the hairpieces as long as they are in keeping with the flowers carried by members of the bridal party. Since it is not always easy to find good artificial blooms, other types of hairpieces may be more satisfactory, durable, and attractive.

How did it go?

Q **My future husband's sister is a very pretty, very thin 21-year-old who's insisting on wearing a strapless, short dress that my friends, who are slightly older and more self-conscious, hate. I want everyone to be comfortable but how do I get her to relent?**

A *She sounds pretty self-absorbed so appeal to her ego. Tell her that your friends are anxious about the comparison and you need to find a compromise for all. Agree that she can have strapless but nix the clingy shift; a structured dress or separates with boning is more accommodating for a range of figures.*

Q **What can I do for my friend who is uncomfortable with her upper arms?**

A *A pretty wrap draped over the shoulders will provide a little extra coverage.*

10

The outlaws

The old adage that you can choose your friends but not your family will never ring so true as in the run up to your wedding – especially when it's other people's family. With the right balance of honesty and firmness, you can cope.

Weddings bring up a lot of intense emotional feelings for all involved, and you may find yourself on the receiving end of some pretty unreasonable demands. Add to this the fact that your own emotions will be running pretty high, and you have a rather volatile situation just waiting to explode.

Often parents may be divorced and sometimes with new partners. All of them will be pressing you to be sensitive to their feelings. They will all feel that they have a special claim on you in some way.

Here's an idea for you... **Invite all of the parents or immediate family out, or round to your house, for dinner. This way they will have some kind of rapport before you get to the big day, and maybe learn to appreciate that there are other close family members who have vested interests.**

BE HONEST

The more you smile and nod whilst secretly plotting to lock your relative in the potting shed, the more complications you make for yourself. A slight smile and shrug will mean that they take for granted your agreement; we all see what we want to when we are looking for it. Try to be friendly but firm from the start. It will be much harder to tell the prospective father-in-law that you don't want his brass band to play marching tunes at the reception if he's already booked it and bought new uniforms to match your bouquet than telling him as soon as the idea is mooted that you'd rather have him charming your guests than stuck behind a euphonium.

MAKE SURE YOU INVOLVE THE SPECIAL PEOPLE

Although you have a guest list to try to manage, be considerate about the others' feelings. You may not know the best friends of your in-laws, but they will have watched your partner grow from being a child and probably been babysitters many times. They will have shared the experience of parenthood with your in-laws and no doubt talked about this moment repeatedly. They are also probably the people listening to the concerns and excitement of your future family regarding the wedding, so if you can possibly include them in some way, it will be no doubt appreciated.

When it comes to family, be clear about their involvement. Ask them what they feel; they may not want to feel like they are adding to your hassles. If you are the bride, ask your fiancé's mum if she would like to come and see

Make sure that whatever problems arise you keep chipper – see IDEA 42, *Arguing*, on making it a happy time.

Try another idea...

the dress or if she wants to help you buy the shoes or accessories. This will be appreciated, even if declined, especially if she doesn't have any daughters of her own. Don't be frightened to bring in the reserves. Ask your mum if she wants to coordinate wedding outfits and you could all shop together for them. You must also ask your partner for help. Make an agreement that you are responsible for difficult discussions with your own families. You don't want to be asking your future father-in-law for deposit cheques.

If they are of a different religion, be sensitive to their requirements. You can ask a celebrant, a respected family figure or a friend of the family to introduce elements of their religious beliefs, such as a blessing, as part of the ceremony. It may mean very little to you if you are of a different religion or an atheist, but a great deal to them. Ask them which part of the ceremony they would feel it is most important to include, and this way they may be more understanding about having to relinquish other elements. If your partner is of a different religion, you may have to consider two ceremonies rather than one. This consideration should stand you in good stead further down the line (like when you are looking for babysitters).

'One would be in less danger
From the wiles of the stranger
If one's kin and kith
Were more fun to be with.'
OGDEN NASH, from *Family Court*

Defining idea...

WHO ARE THEY?

Are the outlaws confident, bold types or are they timid people eager to please? Make sure that you really do consider precisely who they are, and don't assume if they're keeping quiet that they are uninterested – they may be trying to avoid adding to your stress. The flip side of this are the very overbearing type of in-laws, who want to force their own vision onto your wedding. You can always tackle this by giving them a part of the wedding to manage that plays to their strengths. Are they great at time keeping, for instance? If so, ask them to organise the cars and transport arrangements.

How did it go?

Q I really like my future mother-in-law but I feel quite remote from her. How do I move our relationship forward before the big day?

A *Consider carefully what kind of person she is. Is she uncomfortable with big displays of affection? Look at the way she treats her son; you may notice that she is not a very tactile person, so don't bombard her. You are marrying her pride and joy, and so you should accept that she will be sizing you up. So use a softly, softly approach. Ask her to go shopping with you and have lunch and go from there.*

Q But I want to feel like she is excited for me at the ceremony. How can I try to enthuse her?

A *She might well already be excited: don't judge her displays of affection by your own standards. At the end of the day, it's better that her affection is hard won and genuine than gushing and two faced.*

11

Coming up roses

Your florist could be your saviour! They may be able to help with more than you think, so learn to ask for what you want and get the best from your blooms.

If the florist keeps pushing you towards arrangements you can't afford, move on. Make sure that you interview them properly, and ask to see their portfolio. If you want to compare prices, choose a simple flower, like a single white rose corsage and a white rose bouquet, and use that as your guide.

A popular, or just good, local florist will know the main venues in the area and should be able to make suitable recommendations. They should also be able to rent table mirrors, vases and candleholders. And it's worth asking if they can provide silk flowers for hair arrangements (or an allergic wedding party member). Some florists charge a fee to deliver flowers to the ceremony and reception sites and to arrange them on site, so check if that is included in your costing.

As well as looking great, you need to consider the fragrance of flowers. Scented flowers on the pews can enhance a spring wedding but can fight the smell of your wedding feast on the buffet tables. And certain flowers look stunning but might not really work in a bouquet or table centre (the lilac globes of alliums are visually arresting, but they are part of the onion family, and smell like it too). Get down to the florist's and familiarise yourself with the scents before you start making decisions about your floral displays.

SO JUST HOW MANY FLOWERS DO YOU NEED?

The bride and her maids aren't the only ones sporting flowers. The groom wears his boutonniére on the left lapel, nearest to his heart. The groom often chooses a flower for his buttonhole that also occurs in the bride's bouquet. To make sure no one mistakes him for the best man (including the bride if she's had a little Dutch courage to steady her nerves), make sure that the groom's arrangement is more elaborate or larger than the other males' buttonholes. The groom gives each man in the wedding party a boutonniére to wear on his left lapel, often including the officiant (if male; a corsage if female).

The groom is also responsible for providing flowers for his mother, the bride's mother, and the grandmothers. Make sure they match the outfit each is wearing. (Ask the chief bridesmaid to find out the colour of each outfit.) He can also win a few points for being exceptionally considerate by planning corsages for the bride's going-away outfit.

As well as people, you have to bring some floral flair to your special occasion. Whether you are in a church or civil ceremony, you will have a main altar where you will be married. As this is one of the most prominent locations for flowers, it's a nice idea to use blooms reflecting the theme or colour of the bride's bouquet. Make sure they are tall or elaborate enough to be seen by guests seated at the back. Check if the church is happy for you to choose your own display, as sometimes you may be expected to have their existing creations, which might clash. Ask if you (or your florist) can talk to the regular flower arranger who can tell you which flowers suit the space and which get lost – some sweet country blooms can seem ineffectual if you are marrying in Westminster Cathedral. You could be better off using two main displays at the altar, rather than the ends of the pews. These are often decorated with flowers, candles, ribbons or pew cards. If your ceremony is outdoors, you could marry under a favourite blossom tree, or hang blooms sewn onto twine from its branches. If it's a winter or autumn wedding, or candlelight ceremony, use candelabra decorated with flowers or greens for a dramatic mood. Obviously, you can add or subtract depending on location and budget.

A strict, limited colour palette can enhance the effect of your flowers, as will choosing a suitable variety of blooms. See IDEA 36, *Choosing a theme for decoration.*

Try another idea...

GETTING A GOOD RECEPTION

The head table is where the wedding party will sit during the reception, and is the most important in terms of decoration. It should be decorated with a dramatic centrepiece to mark it out from the others. As it is often a rectangular shape, it looks wonderful with garlands draped around the edges, which also allows guests to see the wedding party. The bridesmaids often place their bouquets in front of their places, so also make this a feature when

'Flowers always make people better, happier and more helpful; they are the sunshine, food and medicine to the soul.'
LUTHER BURBANK, naturalist

Defining idea...

planning. The guest tables often have flower arrangements. These need to be low enough for the guests to chat over, or high enough for them to see through (like large fluted vases).

If you are having buffet tables use floral tables to keep them in theme with the rest of the room. Use the food to its best advantage, too, such as piling fruit like a cornucopia, adding to the feeling of celebration. Think laterally: pumpkins might sound like a strange choice but can be striking as part of an autumnal display, as can herbs.

How did it go?

Q   I love flowers and don't want to skimp on them, but my quote from the florist had me reaching for the smelling salts. I've decided not to decorate the church but can't find anywhere else I'm willing to miss out. Any ideas?

A   *There are lots of ways round this. Ask your florist to come up with a similar arrangement but supplementing some of the flowers with more readily available, less expensive blooms. As long as you are willing to budge on the flowers you choose, any florist worth their salt should be able to do this.*

Q   What if I don't want to change to more affordable flowers?

A   *Consider doing the table centres for the reception yourself, or enlist a talented friend or relative. An elegant, tightly packed head of roses in a plain vase can be very effective; just remember this will take a bit of time. And don't skimp on your bouquet or anything vital and elaborate.*

12

The bouquets

The bouquet needs considering almost as soon as your dress, and choosing the right one will be essential to the success of the overall effect of your wedding day look.

Hopefully, by now, you have an idea of what kind of wedding you want. Is it a romantic vintage inspired do, or a very Modern Millie affair? Your bouquet should be a perfectly distilled version of this theme, whilst complementing your look (and, if you are very clever, your figure too).

First you need a suitable partner in crime. It's time to bring in your florist: you need to ensure that you are, ahem, singing from the same hymn book. If you do not feel a rapport with your florist, or they are trying to force their vision onto you rather than letting you call the shots, move on. They may want a chance to recreate the Eiffel Tower in carnations but unless that's your dream too, you can say 'no'. That said, a good florist should be able to guide a confused bride towards their dream

Here's an idea for you...

The orange blossom is the original bridal bloom, symbolising beauty, personality and fertility for hundreds of years. But there are many other ways to florally express your feelings for your loved one. Learn how to use the language of flowers:

Almond blossom, hope; **Apple blossom**, good fortune; **Camellia**, gratitude; **Carnation**, fascination; **Chrysanthemum (red)**, I love you; **Chrysanthemum (white)**, truth; **Cyclamen**, modesty; **Daffodil**, regard; **Daisy**, innocence; **Gardenia**, joy; **Heather**, good luck; **Heliotrope**, devotion; **Honeysuckle**, generosity; **Hyacinth**, loveliness; **Iris**, burning love; **Ivy**, fidelity; **Japonica**, loveliness; **Jasmine**, amiability; **Lemon blossom**, fidelity in love; **Lilac**, youthful innocence; **Lily**, majesty; **Magnolia**, perseverance; **Mimosa**, sensitivity; **Orange blossom**, purity; **Orchid**, beauty; **Peach blossom**, captive; **Rose**, love and happiness; **Snowdrop**, hope; **Sweet pea**, pleasure; **Violet**, faithfulness.

blooms by asking a few pertinent questions. Always take along reference material (don't worry if it's inconsistent, you can talk that through too) and be open to their ideas. That is, after all, what you are paying them for. If you have any doubts, however, always ask if you can call back the next day; a bit of space will let you see if those ideas were exactly what you want, or exactly what you think you should have. It is also easy to get carried away in the moment, so be wary. And don't forget to ask if they can preserve your bouquet should you choose to.

LET'S BEGIN

There is no set way to do this, but you need to start somewhere, so make it colour, shape, flower or theme. Traditionally a bridal bouquet is made of white flowers, but few brides stick to that rule. If you do want to do that, a nice way to bring colour in is to have your bridesmaid's bouquet made up in a smaller version, using the same flower but in a colour. (With grown-up bridesmaids, you may want to opt for wrist corsages instead, or vary the colours.) If you want to choose your bouquet by colour, or a mix of complementary colours, your florist should be able to present you with a selection of blooms available in those shades. The main shapes are a loose and hand tied arrangement, a flowing cascade (which is full at

See IDEA 18, *Crowning glory*, for how flowers can be used to great effect in your hair.

Try another idea...

the top and trails to a point), a tight cluster, a pomander (a ball of flower heads carried by a ribbon) or a nosegay or basket filled with flowers, or arm bouquet that rests naturally in the crook of the arm. You may have a love of a certain flower that you want to build your bouquet around, or be holding a 1920s themed wedding, in which case flowers popular in that era, like Calla lilies, are a good choice.

HELPING YOU BLOOM

The bride usually holds flowers at waist height, and this needs to figure in your plan. If you are petite, an overwhelming cascade bouquet will overpower you (and possibly tip you over), so choose something in proportion to your size. Similarly, if you have a fuller figure, a small pomander might look a bit inconsequential whereas a cascade will lengthen your silhouette. As with your dress, keep an open mind about the shape you want until you have explored the options. The colour you choose must also flatter your skin tone, especially if you intend to also have them in your hair. Whatever you choose needs to work with the flow of your dress and not obscure you – this is decoration, not camouflage.

'There are always flowers for those who want to see them.'
HENRI MATISSE

Defining idea...

FORGET ME NOT

Smell is the most evocative of the senses, and the most likely to trigger memories, so include a scented bloom. A lovely way to make your flowers special to you for more than just the day is to choose seasonal blooms, so that the daffodils will always remind you of your spring wedding (and hopefully remind your groom that your anniversary is nigh). Another advantage of choosing seasonal blooms is that they will be able to withstand the weather conditions. If your bouquet includes delicate flowers that can wilt, make sure your arrangement can incorporate a bouquet holder to keep them fresh – your hand-tied posy won't look quite so great if it's turning brown at the edges. If you want exotic or off-season flowers, make sure this is discussed well in advance. And make sure you are clear about whether the flowers are to be collected or delivered, and at what time.

How did it go?

Q   I'm a bit of a tomboy and feel uncomfortable with flowers. Do I have to have them?

A   *You may find yourself unsure what to do with your hands, so do carry something. Consider a single stem or a little handbag with a bloom through the clasp.*

Q   How can I get over feeling all girlie and self-conscious?

A   *Look for something with a bit of attitude and wit. Try using a thick, soft velvet ribbon, a collar of net or lace or a frill of grass to add some structure.*

Something old...

No, not your gran, but a guide to wedding traditions and their origination. Just why do you need to wear something blue, and why shouldn't the bride walk over the threshold?

There are many customs and superstitions associated with weddings. In the past a wedding was seen as a time when people were particularly susceptible to bad luck and evil spirits and the rituals were supposed to help. They can be fun, too.

You may be the most practical and level-headed of people, but remember that most people enjoy indulging in the rituals and customs of weddings. Even weddings incorporating religious or cultural differences can join in the fun. Make your own rules and put together a combination that means something to you as a couple.

It seems to be that although we still practise these customs few people know what they symbolise, beyond 'good luck'. Here are some pointers.

Here's an idea for you... **If you have different faiths marrying, think how to incorporate traditions from both. As well as good fun, they will get guests talking to each other about what the traditions mean. They are also a great way to make families feel recognised if you are having a non-denominational ceremony.**

WHO'S NEXT?

Every woman knows the meaning of tossing the bridal bouquet: whoever catches the bouquet is the next to be married. If you want to keep the bouquet as a memento, have a smaller, less expensive bouquet specifically made for aiming at your best friend. Let's just hope she isn't pushed to the ground in the scramble. If she is, she gets another chance with the throwing of the garter. This is not just a cheeky chance to show the assembled wedding party that you are wearing stockings, it was originally meant to keep back the guests who were overly anxious to disrobe the newlyweds as they made it to their bed. A parallel custom is for the groom to remove the garter worn by the bride and throw it back over his shoulder toward the unmarried guests. Again the one who catches it will be the next to marry.

'SOMETHING OLD, SOMETHING NEW, SOMETHING BORROWED, SOMETHING BLUE...'

...And the final line many forget from this Victorian rhyme: 'And a silver sixpence in your shoe'. The 'something old' refers to the past, the couple's family and friends. The 'new' is their new life as a couple. The 'something borrowed' is often lent by the bride's family and is an item much valued by the family (hopefully not a grand piano) and must be returned for her good luck to be collected. 'Something blue' is an ancient Israelite custom: the bride wore a blue ribbon in her hair to represent fidelity. The sixpence in the bride's shoe was to ensure wealth in the couple's married life. Although you can use modern currency if you are clean out of sixpences, it's probably best to stay away from some of today's plate-size coins. The garter is often given to represent one of these items too.

Like the symbolism of traditions? See IDEA 12, *The bouquets*, and learn how to say it with flowers, symbolically.

Try another idea...

DRESSING THE PART

This has always been very important. However, white wedding dresses are a new invention; many brides wore coloured dresses in times gone by. The rich started the tradition of white, which symbolises maidenhood, in the sixteenth century. Despite its pretty, irreverent use these days, the veil, which became popular in the UK in the eighteenth century, was originally worn by Roman brides as a camouflage to disguise the bride from evil spirits. This is also why bridesmaids were dressed in a similar way to the bride – they were decoys. It's not very often that you get to ask your mates to act as your protectors against the powers of evil sprits, so enjoy it. However, the etiquette of how to handle them getting the bad luck that was aimed at you is unclear. Maybe you could buy them a bottle of wine.

Strangely, shoes have also played a big part in weddings. The bride's father used to give the groom a pair of the bride's shoes to symbolise the passing of responsibility for the daughter to the husband; a modern version of this could be the handing over of her unpaid Visa bill which she ran up buying shoes. Even the throwing of

'Tradition is a guide and not a jailer.'
W. SOMERSET MAUGHAM

Defining idea...

53

the bouquet over the shoulder was originally performed by her throwing one of her shoes over her shoulder; if they are expensive, however, be prepared not to get them back. And, of course, shoes are still tied to the back of the wedding car for good luck.

We can thank the Italians for confetti, which translates into sweets, which are thrown over the couple after the ceremony and symbolise prosperity and fertility.

The final tradition, which has been seen in thousands of Hollywood weepies, is the carrying of the bride over the threshold. The fact that she usually has been paying her share of the mortgage on that threshold for some time is neither here nor there. After the wedding, the groom is supposed to carry the bride over the threshold when they enter the marital home for the first time. One explanation is that the bride will suffer bad luck if she falls when passing over the threshold or enters with her left foot first. She can thus avoid both dangers by being carried. The modern explanation is that she may just be a bit too merry to make it home on her own.

Q **Since I was a child, my mother, who's a strict Catholic, has always told me that she'd like me to wear her family heirloom, a garter, at my own wedding. I'm having a pagan ceremony, though, and feel like a fraud. How can I say no?**

How did it go?

A *Why do you have to? Although the rhyme is Victorian, the traditions that surround weddings are from much earlier; so much so that we are unsure of the origins of most of them.*

Q **So can I adopt other traditions too? I've always loved the Jewish breaking of the glass.**

A *Well, you will need to put your own spin on it, or acknowledge its origins so you don't offend any Jewish guests, but why not? It's your day, so have it your way.*

TO DO :

> TURN IN RECEIPTS
> PACK FOR N.Y.
> GET CASH
> PICK-UP PLANE TICKET
> INVOICE NAPLES INDUSTRIES
> CALL JODI
> CALL MARSHA RE: COMMISSION
> TAX W-9 FORM
> B-DAY PRESENT BROOKS
> DROP DRY CLEANING
> CELL PHONE BATTERY
> BUSINESS MAP·
> PROPERTY RELEASE FORMS ⟨TOWN TOWER⟩
> DISC & SOFTWARE BOOKS
> SPREAD SHEETS FOR ICON GRAPHICS
> FILM
> TIME CARDS
> STAMPS
> LANNY'S B-DAY FRAME
> NEW LICENSE PLATES
> DOG FOOD FOR MAX & SOCKS
> ...NGE OIL & BRAKE FLUID

14

How to say 'I don't' and 'you do'

The key to a happy wedding, a sane bride and a wedding that won't be annulled is to master two ancient and rare arts: saying 'no' and delegation.

If you can share responsibility and refuse to take on too much, it will stop you from cracking under the pressure, and it may also allow you a little time to sit back and enjoy the ride.

Finding suppliers, venues, a reliable and tasteful caterer: the things-to-do list can seem endless. However, you have a much bigger resource at your hands than you think. How many of your friends are already married? Ask them about their disasters as well as their triumphs, and collect their recommendations. Get all the names and numbers you can from them.

If you have friends who are especially good at certain tasks, tell them that you admire their talents, and then enlist their help. Got a shopaholic sister? Tell her you need her help to find silver ballet shoes for the flower girls in miniature sizes and

Here's an idea for you... **Design a spreadsheet with names and contact details alongside the delegated list of tasks. Post it on the web so people can access it, or print it out and hand copies to all concerned so they can coordinate if necessary.**

watch her go. This isn't really manipulation, just an efficient way of getting the best out of everyone whilst making them feel good about it. And if someone has a task they enjoy, they are much more likely to excel at it.

By the same token, a night in with some fountain pens, a bottle of wine and your mum will give her a warm glow of being involved, and a chance to get all those invitations addressed. Then there will be all the RSVPs to deal with; so you need to ask people to chip in there, as there will be a lot of chasing. Perhaps one of the bridesmaids can be given this as a single responsibility; it is a big job and one that can become more complex if you try to split it.

Rather than being a huge burden, asking for help can be a great way of including slightly marginalized people, such as a favourite aunt, who has no official position but would like to be involved. Make sure that you show appreciation to whomever you ask, and don't dump a dull task on somebody while you skip off with the bridesmaids shopping for underwear and a long boozy lunch. Most people will be happy to help if they feel appreciated.

Now you have to start saying no. You must set out clear boundaries with all involved so when you hear the words 'Oh, I'm busy, can you do it?' you are very clear that, no, you can't. Do not explain why not; just be firm. It may seem tough to start with, but the more you do it the easier it gets, and it will save you a lot of problems, and resentment, further down the line.

Find it hard to say no? Get yourself a wedding coordinator who can take over the tough bit of putting up boundaries. Your mother-in-law may find it acceptable to bully you into matching thrones at the reception but the professional distance a wedding coordinator can bring will make it impossible for her to win.

Want to make sure that your partner understands how much there is to do? Make them read IDEA 50, *Time lines*, so they get with the programme.

Try another idea…

Don't micromanage everything. The key to successful delegation is trust, so do not peer over people's shoulders, metaphorically or physically. The classic way to de-motivate someone is to check up on him or her all the time. It is reasonable to ask for a progress report but appreciate that other people have lives and that your wedding isn't the centre of theirs like it is yours. Try not to delegate anything time sensitive, like booking the church or reception.

Many hotel venues have wedding organisers who are on hand during the day, so find out how much you can rely on them and what they are responsible for. Will they be on hand to let in the florists? Do they oversee the setting up of the bar and putting favours on tables? Clear this up as soon as you start discussions, or you could end up duplicating work. You may also need to ask your bridesmaids to have a spot check on the day. If you are planning on doing some of the catering or table displays yourself, make sure that someone else is overseeing the final implementation when the big day arrives. If you give yourself too much to think about, it will end up feeling like you've thrown a great party but you didn't get to enjoy it.

'The art of leadership is saying no, not yes. It is very easy to say yes.'
TONY BLAIR

Defining idea…

59

If someone else in your party is overseeing aspects such as the flowers, make sure that they come to the meetings with you so that they know exactly what they are meant to be doing, and what things are meant to look like. Many a disaster has occurred when two people interpreted the same set of words in different ways.

How did it go?

Q   I think about all the details of the planning constantly. No one seems to be helping and time is running out. How can I fire them up?

A   *Sounds like you are running on Bride Time. To other people, six months away sounds like a lifetime, but you want to tick things off the list now. You need to be patient with them but explain your concerns firmly to turn up their sense of urgency.*

Q   But I feel like no one cares and I am the only one taking this seriously. What if they just tell me that I'm being overly worried?

A   *It is a simple case of getting your communication right. Explain to your helpers how stressed you feel rather than pointing the finger of blame (or you'll find them even less willing to help). Let them know that the sooner these things are taken care of, the sooner will come the time that you can relax and enjoy the run up to your big day.*

15

Smile!

One thing is for sure, your big day will pass in a complete blur and seem to last four minutes rather than twenty-four hours. So, you will be relying heavily on your photographs and video to remind you that you didn't just dream the whole thing.

When you start looking for your photographer, you should cast your net wide and see as many portfolios as you have time for. Remember, there is only one chance to capture the magic of this day, so you need the right eye behind the lens.

There is a huge range of styles and options to consider, and making the right choice means that you will be able to reflect the very personal feel of your own day. With that in mind, you will by now be aware that there are a lot of other people to consider – you may want more reportage-style shots whereas older family members want more posed, traditional shots as mementos of the day. It is a good idea to set

Here's an idea for you...

It's common to have a videographer at weddings too, and if they are filming digitally they can often produce great stills as well as videos. Look at their show reel (their version of a photographer's portfolio) to see what they can do.

aside some time before your reception to make sure that everyone has the combination they would like. (Make sure you order extra sets of these prints for sending out; putting them in a frame as special gifts for grandparents would be a nice touch.) Brides sometimes like to have a posed portrait before the wedding, so do ask if that is available too.

KEEPING IT STRICTLY BUSINESS

Be wary of allowing eager amateurs to help out. Specialised wedding photographers will understand wedding procedures, ceremonies and receptions, so they can anticipate your next move and be in the proper place at the right time to capture all the special moments. Make sure that your photographer is someone you feel comfortable with; if they remind you of a sergeant major and your dream wedding is more along the lines of Glastonbury, but with more mud, you will clash terribly. Make sure they are happy to cajole merry family members along for the group shots and can keep things moving along. Imagine how devastated you would be if your cousin's kind-hearted attempt to help went wrong and you had no decent pictures of the day.

Look at his or her work. See if the photographer captured the excitement and emotion of the bridal couple. Don't be frightened to take along pages torn from magazines or photographs you have that capture a feel that you like. It is also reasonable to ask them about their attire: they may think that trainers are acceptable or come in full morning suit, so check. Also check if they bring an assistant with them, and enquire after their attire too.

EXTRAS! EXTRAS!

Once you like someone's style, you need to clear up a few grey areas. This is where some less reputable photographers make their money. How much do extra prints cost? Is processing included in the cost? Who gets the negatives, you or them? Many photographers keep the rights to the negatives, so you can only get extra prints through them. If so, see if you can negotiate a fee to release them to you after a certain time. Ask the photographer how soon after the wedding you will get the prints. You should also ask if they could do retouching. A good photographer should have liability insurance, offer a money-back guarantee and make references available if you require them.

In terms of style, it's often nice to get reportage shots of the bride in preparation before the ceremony, so consider whether or not you would be comfortable with a male photographer catching you or your fiancé in your smalls. Be clear about the amount of time you expect them to spend at the wedding, and if you want them at the reception. In case things run over, check what the cost per additional hour of shooting would be. A good photographer will be prepared for this eventuality, and not skip out before you are happy. Be wary of booking someone who has booked a second wedding later that day. It's just an added pressure for you and will prevent them from being entirely focused on your day.

Photographs can make a great 'thank you' for nearest and dearest. IDEA 27, *Thank yous and gifts*, shows you how.

Try another idea...

'*We do not remember days, we remember moments.*'
CESARE PAVESE, Italian novelist

Defining idea...

63

FEELING GOOD

You will be expected to select the finish for the printed pictures, which are usually gloss or matt. There is a huge range of effects that can alter the way your photographs look and feel, such as adding a white border or making a small print on a large sheet of paper. The photographer should also be able to offer your colour prints in sepia or black and white, but remember that they will not have the same level of contrast as photographs taken in black and white film. Ask your photographer to shoot using both types of film if possible. Don't forget to check if you need to order extras for family and friends.

How did it go?

Q   The vicar says we can't have any photographs! What can I do about it?

A   Make sure you understand exactly what he is saying; many vicars are simply referring to the obtrusive flash photography by some over-eager amateur photographers.

Q   Can the vicar stop us?

A   Well, you could do it anyway but annoying the vicar wouldn't set a very nice tone. It is vital that your photographer understands the rules and regulations of your church before planning the ceremony shots. Some churches do not allow photographs to be taken during the ceremony, but most allow shots before and after.

16

Make an entrance

How do you imagine your big entrance? Helicopter or horse and carriage? Or are you so in love you are just going to sprint to the church? Get there in style, and on time.

As sexist as this is going to sound, the fact is, if you want the groom to pull his weight in the preparations, the best thing to do is give him something he might enjoy sorting out, like the transport. Of course, it might be the bride that's the petro-head, but there does tend to be a grain of truth in any stereotype.

If you want to keep the wedding vehicles a surprise, start by talking themes. Vintage or modern? Four legged or two wheeled? Also, there are a few practicalities to consider before you commit. An open-top, low-slung Jaguar could look incredibly chic and fitting if the bride is wearing a sharp cream trouser suit. However, the same bride, in a huge skirt and petticoats, would look like an upside down

A white car can make cream or ivory dresses look dirty in photographs, so compare scraps of sample fabric against the car to check for a clash. If you are not sure what you are looking for, it works like this: a 'warm' white or cream has a yellow undertone; a cold white has a 'blue' undertone. The two together clash. Different shades can go together as long as they are both 'warm' or both 'cold'.

lampshade after she'd squeezed through the door. Same bride, white '60s style mini dress and huge veil – she'll need the veil to cover her mortified blushes after displaying more than she'd like to the assembled wedding party as she climbs in. It won't be a great wedding night if the bride has been humiliated, purposefully or not.

This is the first step on your life's biggest journey, so get it right. Do you want something to remind you of the era you were married in? A white Bentley may be a classic choice, but what about a sky blue Mini for that something blue? You might also want the close family in matching transport that could make for a grand exit. A little thought makes the difference between adding another special part to the day and something perfunctory that drearily gets you from A to B.

CHECK IT OUT

Make sure you go and see the cars, as a brochure or web site can be deceptive. Are they well maintained, will it be used by other weddings that day and, if so, will they valet it in between so the bride doesn't turn up with other people's confetti on her dress? Do they include the ribbons and flowers; can you be involved in choosing them or selecting something different? You may want to carry the theme of the wedding flowers through.

There are other options that don't involve petrol, such as ones that involve aviation fuel. A small plane or helicopter would be a memorable way to leave your guests, and get hats fluttering. This could be less expensive than you might think.

Make sure your transport suits the theme. Look at IDEA 36, *Choosing a theme for decoration.*

Try another idea...

Some prefer the four-legged way of getting around on their big day. However, if you are shy you might want to reconsider, as it's not exactly speedy. And a horse and carriage is not suitable for getting you long distances across town in the rush hour. If you don't have far to go to reach your reception, consider having the bride riding side-saddle as you lead her on a horse – a pretty romantic gesture. You might give up on transport altogether, if your reception is nearby, and stroll with your wedding party in a grand procession. A nice touch here would be to provide some pretty parasols against summer sun for your beloved and your attendants (and grannies and mums), or some umbrellas to be carried by the ushers just in case.

'Take most people, they're crazy about cars. I'd rather have a goddamn horse. A horse is at least human, for God's sake.'
J. D. SALINGER

Defining idea...

Whatever you decide to do, you need to book well in advance, perhaps even a year before, especially if you are looking at a Saturday in the summer. If you can't get the car you want through a hire agency, try approaching a classic car or collectors club. Don't forget to reconfirm and check your route by driving it in advance. It would be a disaster if you give everybody a route taken from a street map which turns out to be all one way; the wrong way. And make sure that everyone knows where the reception is – don't rely on convoys as they only ever work if no one else is on the road. You can always have extra reception cards on hand with one of the ushers in case of emergency (someone is bound to have forgotten them). Also make sure someone has a cab number in case of rain emergencies.

How did it go?

Q   I've booked our wedding car, and now she tells me I have to do all the others. What others?

A   It is the groom's responsibility, although often the best man will help, to book cars for both sets of parents, your attendants, and of course, one to take you to the airport or your first-night hotel. You may also want to include other close family members such as grandparents in that equation. And don't forget, cars are needed to collect everyone and take them to the ceremony, and then take them to the reception.

Q   Blimey. Sounds expensive. Is there anything I can do to rein in the costs?

A   It's not necessarily a fortune. You often can book by the hour, and if you don't want a whole row of priceless white vintage Fords you can have a set of sleek black London-style cabs that look elegant (but make sure that they are not emblazoned with ads when booking). What about a London bus for the second stage of the journey? Use your imagination, not just your chequebook.

17

Where: choosing a location

A location must be more than a pretty backdrop for the photos. It will have a direct influence on how many guests you can invite, the kind of entertainment you can have, and whether or not you can do a full waltz for your first dance.

For most, a key consideration in deciding on the 'where' will be your budget limitations. But that doesn't mean you can't have some fun; there is still lots of scope within that for some imagination.

Think bigger than the local church: what about a cathedral with spires and stained glass, a glamorous hotel ballroom, a public park, a rooftop, marrying on holiday or even your own back garden strewn with a hundred balloons? There are endless possibilities, so don't just opt for the obvious without a little research.

WHERE TO START

What will suit the kind of ceremony and reception you want? Your location should be a reflection of your overall theme. If it's formal, your local grand hotel may be a

Here's an idea for you... **Outdoor ceremony or reception? Make a plan to enclose 'If rain stops play...' cards with your invites, informing guests of an alternative location in case of bad weather. It might simply mean moving to a room inside the hotel or, if you are marrying at home with a garden reception, a local pub. Just make sure the wording is clear – you don't want to lose half your guests to the King's Arms when they should be at the King's Head.**

possibilities, so don't just opt for the obvious without a little research.

WHERE TO START

What will suit the kind of ceremony and reception you want? Your location should be a reflection of your overall theme. If it's formal, your local grand hotel may be a suitable location (and should be licensed for civil weddings), with plenty of space for ceremony and guests. But make sure you have free rein to make your own choices – they sometimes insist on using their own favoured caterer. And check there's enough parking space.

If you plan to hold a church wedding, you may need to book up to two years in advance for the date that you want. If you want something a little more unusual, such as a ceremony with your own vows in a ruined castle, try a quiet registry office and a second ceremony; that way you are free to make all your own style choices.

Make sure you have a dry run well in advance of the big day. You must make sure that you know which door the band will use, and that they also know which one it is, unless you want everyone moving tables to allow equipment to be lugged through your reception meal. Will the fire regulations allow for the hundreds of tea lights you have planned to dot all around your tables? Is there room for you to greet your guests? Can they make sure that there is a safe place for the wedding gifts to be left, or can they be locked away and collected the following day by your parents if you are going on honeymoon straight from the reception?

ALL THE HELP YOU CAN GET

The first question that you ask of the person who manages your venue (even if it's your mum and her back garden) is 'What exactly can you do for me?' If you are opting for a more traditional venue, there should be several resources on hand: the church might take care of the altar flowers, a hotel might have a valet who can handle the parking, a banqueting hall might have a toastmaster that they can recommend. The added bonus of following recommendations is that these people will have worked together before and already be familiar with the way things run. One less thing to tick off your list.

Hotels will sometimes offer the use of extra rooms, or even discounts on group bookings for the wedding party, so it's worth asking. Make sure you keep asking. Even if you are marrying a sports buff and holding your reception in the cricket club, they may be more than happy to string the place with bunting or put your names on the scoreboard. You will also find that quite quickly your organisational list becomes very long, so clear up the areas of responsibility early; if the venue has a great relationship with a reliable cab firm why worry about tracking one down yourself? Local knowledge is a wonderful thing.

Try another idea…

As you are choosing the venue, consider the time of day that you are hoping to marry and hold your reception. A medieval banqueting room might look a bit bleak and lost in the middle of the day, but at night will come alive with warming points of flickering candlelight. See **IDEA 2, *When: date and time*,** for more ideas.

Defining idea…

'*Luck is being in the right place at the right time, but location and timing are to some extent under our control.*'
NATASHA JOSEFOWITZ, US script writer

71

How did it go?

Q **I went to my local church as a child and it would be very special for me to get married there, but there is nowhere nearby to hold the reception – it's all very rural. Is it unreasonable for guests to travel 40 minutes to a decent venue?**

A *It depends on how you expect them to get there. You could take the stress out of it by hiring a couple of old fashioned buses and ushering the guests onto them. Keep the festive feel by adorning them with ribbons and balloons.*

Q **But what about the guests collecting their cars later?**

A *Well, those not drinking would probably prefer to drive themselves to the reception anyway. Have a good think about alternatives. Is there a nice meadow nearby, owned by a friendly farmer who might be willing to let you set up a marquee? If it is very close by, you could even make a nice show of a good old-fashioned wedding procession. Just remember you will need generators for power, unless you are going to go very rural and just stick to candlelight (not advised in a marquee). And check the field for bulls.*

18

Crowning glory

Some things are a matter of life and death; some are more important – like gorgeous hair. And that isn't achieved overnight. Take responsibility for looking fabulous.

You can spend all the money in the world on good cuts, but if you don't give your hair the appropriate TLC in between you won't get the results you hope for.

From the minute the engagement ring is slipped on your finger, you need to start getting serious about your mane. Take the time to work out your hair type (ask your hairdresser if you aren't sure) and start using the appropriate shampoo and conditioner and a weekly treatment pack.

Bear in mind that getting your hair into its premium condition isn't just about splashing out on the products (and splashing them on). Have your hair trimmed regularly to guard against split ends (ideally every six weeks; if you find yourself fiddling with them while you are on the phone, you've left it too long) and avoid overusing heated appliances and styling aids. Consider giving your hair a 'day off' every week. Consider hiding it under a cute headscarf on a Sunday: after all, do you

Here's an
idea for
you...

Little bridesmaids or flower girls often wear a wreath of flowers as a hairpiece, and can look adorable in them – if you can get them to keep them on. If they are very young and have silky and fine hair, have the flowers made into a crown to rest on the hair with slides or grips. This is where your maid of honour comes in: make her responsible for carrying a damage limitation kit, including hairspray and spare grips for all, to protect against mishaps and the elements.

really need to straighten it to within an inch of its life whilst you wash the car or do a supermarket run?

ATTACK OF THE WEDDING RINGLETS

You probably should head straight for the salon anyway, but if you've had a skinhead on a playful whim and you want an up-do for your big day, you need a plan, and fast. Hairdressers can always tell that your fantasy style will make you look like an extra from Dallas, and how long it will take (at least a year to six months if you need to grow out a fringe or a perm). If you are thinking of any radical changes, consider doing it now so that there's still plenty of time to limit the damage if you then decide it's really not you. And try to avoid the strange phenomenon that is wedding ringlets – you might be unpleasantly surprised how they can sneak up on you. Although no grown woman sports them in normal life, a flick through any wedding photographer's portfolio will show a rash of them.

When you have ordered your dress, show a picture to the hairdresser and see if they agree that your chosen style will work with your neckline. About six weeks before the wedding, book a practice session with your hairdresser, taking any tiara, headdress, hat or veil you might have. If you're going to wear a veil and you plan to take it off during the day, let them know, as your style needs to be able to stay intact and still look elegant.

Wash your hair the night before your wedding – freshly washed hair is hard to work with especially if you intend to put it up. Get friendly with styling products, and don't leave it until the last minute to try them out; there are many different ones to choose from and your hair type will suit certain brands better than others. You can also easily overload hair by using too much or not get the result you want by being too timid. Practice here is key.

Your bridesmaids' styles need to reflect the general theme of your wedding. Try a night of pampering together, to talk through ideas that everyone can be comfortable with. Take a look at IDEA 9, *Ladies in waiting.*

Try another idea...

And remember, have colour treatments or perms done a few weeks in advance to allow them to settle down (no one wants the stench of perming fluid wafting down the aisle as you do).

HONEYMOON HAIR

Depending on your honeymoon location, it's unlikely that your honeymoon hair is going to resemble your wedding 'display'. More often than not, you will be tackling a whole new set of challenges, such as sun damage, chlorine and humidity. And there is little reason to spend months getting your hair in shape before the big day only to let it flop as soon as you've said 'I (up) do'. Surely you should wait until at least the first anniversary to let yourself go. Make sure you pack the appropriate products to combat the stresses to tresses.

'And forget not that the earth delights to feel your bare feet and the winds long to play with your hair.'
KAHLIL GIBRAN

Defining idea...

75

How did it go?

Q   I'm utterly distressed – my hair is falling out and it's gone dull and miserable. And I've been nurturing it better than any time before in my whole life but it's never looked worse! What's going on?

A   *It's probably stress. Give yourself a day off, do something entirely unrelated to weddings and treat yourself to a reconditioning and strengthening treatment. You also probably need a good boost of vitamin B to help beat the stress too.*

Q   But what about the shedding? My hair feels so thin.

A   *Don't panic, we can rebuild her. When you condition, keep conditioner to a minimum so you don't weigh it down. Wash the night before, and on the big day use volumising spray. If it really is very thin, consider wearing your hair up; and don't be frightened of a little backcombing to add body and staying power. Just remember to smooth it over, or you might look a little frightened.*

19

Get glowing

Even if you think of yourself as a natural kind of girl, to get away with the bare minimum on the day will still probably take a lot of planning beforehand. The good news is that you'll have a legitimate reason for pampering yourself.

It's always a good idea to get on first name terms with your beauty therapist. She can help you get some understanding of your body and cycles. Do you have any particular triggers that give you problems?

The first tip for great skin couldn't be simpler. Everyone needs to drink more water – it's not hard to get hold of and it will help clear your complexion. Good basic skin care is also a must, so make sure you cleanse, tone and moisturise morning and night. Use products designed for your skin type (most beauty counters offer a free type analysis, so seek them out if you are unsure). Facial exfoliators will help to make skin more radiant so use one at least once a week. For serious problems, or

Here's an idea for you...

Get your hands in shape. Not only will your hands be shaken and kissed, but also your new sparklers will be admired. The last thing that you need is to try to show off your ring with the claws of a crone. Make sure you keep a hand and nail treatment cream by your bed to keep them in tip top condition. And don't forget that pedicure.

ones that don't respond to these routines, visit your doctor and ask them to refer you to a dermatologist. Now is also the time to tackle any dental issues you want to address, as a treatment plan could take some time.

IT'S YOUR DUTY TO TREAT YOURSELF

Treat yourself to a monthly facial, and plan the timing so any eruptions caused as the skin begins to renew itself don't happen near the big day. It will also help calm your nerves and create a bit of vital personal time that will help keep you balanced. It is also important to splash out on some new pampering products, such as new make-up, fragrances and lush body cream. It will help to make you feel special and suitably princess-like.

PUT ON A HAPPY FACE

This is a perfect opportunity to give your look a real overhaul. Many women stick to the habits they formed as a teenager, which may have worked well for some time, but our skin texture, face shape and pallor change throughout our lives and, therefore, so will the colours and styles that suit us.

You should think about this at least several weeks, preferably months, before your wedding. You need to get used to the new you, and other people need time to do so too. After all, you don't want to look like a stranger walking down the aisle. Get the professionals in if you are unsure. You can always have a make-up lesson, or head once again to your department store's beauty counter. Make sure they know you want a bridal look and are not planning to do a rain dance. If you will be doing your make-up on the big day, it's best to keep your colours fairly neutral and make sure it's something you feel you can replicate. If your bridesmaids will be making you up, take them to the store with you.

Why not use your treatment times as a way to involve your in-laws, or relatives who don't have any special role, by asking them to come along with you. Or see IDEA 27, *Thank yous and gifts*, for ideas about how to make them feel special.

Try another idea...

Even if you don't normally wear make-up, you might want to consider it for your nuptials. Flash photography can be very unflattering and bleach the colour from anyone; even a touch of foundation can even out your complexion to great effect.

Have a complete run through of your make-up from start to finish so that you can gauge exactly how much time you will need to allow on the day, and make sure you do any eyebrow plucking the day before, so you don't have an unpleasant, red Vulcan v between your eyes.

If you have a facial in the week before your wedding, don't try anything new as you could have a reaction. On the day, stick to your practised routine and don't deviate from it; you could create a monster you don't know how to repair. Make sure someone close to you, physically and emotionally, carries some touch-up products and is on hand to help you when you might be expected to look particularly fabulous.

'Beauty is in the heart of the beholder.'
AL BERNSTEIN

Defining idea...

Q   **I'm someone whose emotions are always written all over her face. And I know I'll be crying like a baby off and on. What can I do?**

A   *You need a waterproof mascara and some make-up pads impregnated with remover tucked in your bridesmaid's handbag, just in case when the flood gates open even the waterproofing can't cope.*

Q   **It gets worse: my neck gets blotchy and bright red. What can I do about that?**

A   *You could get away with a green tinged concealer from a regular make-up brand, but you may have to go for some serious coverage. Try stage make-up, or make-up designed for scar coverage that has special green pigmentation to neutralise redness. Make sure you brush with loose powder to fix it afterwards.*

20

The body beautiful

There are some women who love their bodies with steadfast conviction. Then there are those of us who are awake. This is the time when most women finally get serious about getting in shape.

Be realistic. How much time have you got? What is achievable? With a combination of diet and exercise, quite a lot, actually.

Don't pin all your hopes on a silk slip designed for a willowy sylph if you're a classic English pear. Instead, choose a gown that plays to your strengths and then work towards that. There have been many disastrous tales of brides who order their dress a size too small only to have to face heading down the aisle like a trussed-up turkey shoved in a carrier bag. So keep it real.

FULL BODIED

A fuller figure that is firm and well looked after is far preferable to a crash diet bag of bones (which can also make your skin's appearance grey and cause energy levels to hit an all-time low). To lose weight you need an exercise regime and a good diet, so plan them properly. Don't set unrealistic Olympian goals with exercise regimes if

Here's an idea for you...

When selecting your wedding fragrance, make sure you can get matching body cream and bath oil; you don't want five fragrances fighting as you lean in to kiss your new husband.

you work long hours, or your failure to stick to them will demoralise and de-motivate you. And get to know your diet weak spots: empty the house of all bad stuff rather than spend all evening trying to resist the siren song of that chocolate in the cupboard, and don't try a diet that insists on fresh seaweed for lunch if you work in the middle of a land locked city centre. The key to success is always suitability.

Don't just try to shed the pounds through diet. If you do, you will miss out on the other main benefits of exercise; namely that it helps to relieve stress and ensures a good night's sleep when you need it most.

DRESSING SLIM

What is your dress like? Ask your gym to create a program that bears that in mind. Maybe you will be wearing a strapless gown, and would like slender, toned arms and shoulders to show off. An A-line dress looks best on trim hips, so make this your target area.

If motivation is a problem, stick a photograph of your dress on the fridge and get yourself a diet buddy; maybe one of the bridesmaids who also wants to shape up for the big event. You can talk each other down from the chocolate biscuit ledge and force each other to the gym – maybe at gunpoint.

If money isn't an issue, then consider paying for a grown-up gym babysitter. A personal trainer will make sure you hit the exercise machines whatever the weather, or favourite TV show repeat. They often charge by the hour so if you can get a couple of others to join in the sessions, you can make it that bit more affordable.

Make your body regime work with your new beauty discipline. Have a look at IDEA 19, *Get glowing*, for suggestions.

Try another idea...

FEELING GOOD

You also want your body to feel sleek and soft to the touch. Keep a bottle of body scrub in the shower so it will quickly become part of your daily routine. Start at your feet and work up the body in small circular motions, always moving towards your heart, and then slather on the body cream. Massage is also good for improving the circulation and expelling toxins from the body, and as a result will improve the look and feel of your skin. Make it an aromatherapy massage for the added benefit of calming and relaxing your slightly frayed soul.

A few days before the wedding, book yourself and your chief bridesmaid or mum into a beauty salon to take care of any waxing and tanning. Fake tans all work differently on different skin types, so try a few before deciding which looks the most natural on you. You need to find out the specifics too: some work best applied on moisturised skin; some 'slip' and cause streaks if applied on top of a body cream. It is advisable to do this a few days before the big day, as they last a few days and it allows a margin for error.

'I always wanted to be somebody, but I should have been more specific.'
JANE WAGNER, playwright

Defining idea...

How did it go?

Q   I'm doing a quickie wedding in Las Vegas and have no time shed the half stone I want to lose. Any quick fixes? I go in a month.

A   A low carbohydrate, high protein diet will help, but you need to couple it with exercise. Walk for half an hour before work (maybe to a further away bus stop), always use stairs (even for ten floors), and use your lunch hour to speed walk around the local park.

Q   I've heard giving up drinking will help weight loss. Is that right?

A   There are a horrifying number of calories in alcohol so definitely shelve it for now. However, you should also get yourself to the gym for a tailored programme and if all else fails get a light fake tan (everyone looks better with a bit of a glow). To be honest, a beaming grin will do far more to make you look like a blooming bride than a diet. That's what everyone will be looking for as you head down the aisle.

21

Grooms grooming

Weddings: they can make a man do the funniest things, like dress up in top hat and tails, and wear moisturiser. This is the chance for more life-style improvements.

Getting married is often a time for evaluation. It's a good chance to think about the past and the future, and where you are at now in the great scheme of things. And wonder where your waistline is going.

Most of us work better with a deadline, so if you have always thought that you would like to regain your slender youth's figure, or try a different hairstyle, why not use this time as an opportunity? It also gives you a chance to muscle in on some of the girls' good stuff. Massages, manicures, and any general chances to be pampered are nothing to be ashamed of if you are simply doing it to look the best for your beloved on the big day. And it feels great.

Here's an idea for you... **Feel unsure about your foray into the world of grooming? Enlist one of your ushers or your best man as a wing man to try these ideas out with. It also means that they won't be able to use it against you at the stag night.**

FIT FOR A KING

You may need to spend a little more time lifting weights, instead of lifting pints. You will know what your body responds to most, but a general rule is cutting back on drinking alcohol, processed food, and upping the exercise quotient. Most men store fat around their waists, so if you want guests whispering about the dash you are cutting, rather than speculating on who the father of your beer pregnancy might be, then there is no other option. Essentially, doing a little exercise does not mean that you can therefore eat what you like – or you won't lose a thing (except the will to live). Visit your gym and ask for a session with a trainer who can create a tailored programme for you, including a sensible diet plan.

DON'T SMILE PLEASE

Do small children run screaming from you in the street when you give them a friendly grin? It may be time to take a trip to the dentist and have a look at your gnashers. For more serious work, you may need to start a dental plan that may take up to at least a year. Whitening can take years off your appearance, as teeth discolour as you age. Don't overdo it though, as you may end up looking like an overgrown Ken doll. And people may be able to see you in the dark.

CLOSE SHAVES AND FINAL CHECKS

If you have ever fancied trying out a good old-fashioned barber's, now is the time. A close shave by a professional, with warm towels to open the pores and a super sharp blade brandished by someone who understands which way the grain goes, is a great way to relax and feel special. See if you can book into a good barber on the morning of the wedding. Some of the grander hotels have them on site, so do check.

You will also need to make some basic checks on the big day. Make sure that you have a brush to remove any specks of lint from your suit. Your shoes need to shine like never before. (Dad in the army? Re-enlist him.) Make sure new underwear and socks are laid out with your new suit, shirt and neck tie the night before. Even your cufflinks should be put out ready so that you don't find yourself on all fours in your new bib and tucker emptying drawers looking for them. Your hands need to be clean, as well as your nails which should also be short as they will be playing a key part in the day. Consider a manicure before the big day so you have less to worry about. If you will be having a haircut, don't do it the day before as it will still have that just scalped look, and don't try anything too radical in case you hate it (twenty-four hours isn't exactly long enough to grow it back).

Make sure that you choose a suit that plays to your strengths. Take a look at IDEA 39, *Choosing a morning suit*, for advice on how to select one.

Try another idea...

'I'm tired of all this nonsense about beauty being only skin-deep. That's deep enough. What do you want, an adorable pancreas?'
JEAN KERR, novelist

Defining idea...

89

How did
it go?

**Q   I always look rubbish in photos, like I've been dug up. I know it
bothers my girlfriend but she pretends it doesn't, although I've
noticed all the pictures she has of me around her flat are black
and white, even if they were taken with colour film. Is there
anything I can do?**

A   *You may be being over-sensitive; she could just be the arty type. Remember
that your professional photographer will have the equipment and skill to
produce top-quality pictures. It would be a good idea to talk to him or her
to raise the problem and learn some tricks of the trade.*

**Q   What could I do to improve the chances of the guests' photos
turning out better? They might look back and think they were at a
zombie wedding.**

A   *OK, you have the unfortunate pallor of a corpse, then. In that case you
need to consider a fake tan, either from a sun bed or out of a bottle. And,
no, it doesn't have to be humiliating. You can now get fake tanning
preparations that don't need a beauty therapist to apply them, as they are
in a spray form and very accurate. If that idea is still a bridge too far, try
buying one you can apply at home from the chemist. If you are
exceptionally pale, try mixing it with a bit of moisturiser first to get a more
subtle result. And do have a test run before the wedding day so you don't
accidentally turn up looking as if you are appearing in panto.*

22

I married a-broad!

People used to run away to Gretna Green to tie the knot; now it tends to be Mauritius or anywhere else with an azure blue sea and some swaying palm trees. If the exotic appeals to you, make sure you understand what it'll mean for your big day.

Who do you want with you on the beach as you say 'I do' under a radiant sun? Will you be husband and wife legally when you get home? What will you wear?

Consider who you would like present, and for how long. For a long-haul destination it is only fair to expect guests to be around for a week, as they will probably have to eat into their annual holiday. You need to allow for this if you are staying in the same destination for your honeymoon (perhaps marry half way through the week so you don't have your new in-laws as chaperones the entire time). Consider the cost of your destination, too; you must be prepared to accept that some guests will be unable to make it due to the expense.

Here's an idea for you... **If you are keen to have guests at your wedding, suggest that they give you their attendance as a wedding gift; flights, hotel rooms and food soon add up, so this could be your way of showing your appreciation.**

'WE'RE NOT RUNNING *FROM*, WE'RE RUNNING *TO*...'

You'll have to handle the announcement of your plans carefully. Some friends and family will be very disappointed, so be prepared to deal with their feelings sensitively. You could take them for a meal or hold a party on your return to give everyone the chance to share your good fortune. Importantly, let them know that you are going away to fulfil a dream, *not* choosing to leave them all behind.

MAKING IT LEGAL

To ensure that your marriage is legal in the UK, you have to be sure that you fit the UK criteria: you must not be underage, awaiting a divorce or married to someone else. To make it legal in your country of choice, then you must ensure that you fit their criteria. It is important to find out the legal requirements. These can include a minimum period of stay in the country (and often a certain number of days before the ceremony can take place). For example, in America you need a blood test, and some countries have religious restrictions. You also need to be aware of the country's public holidays and festivals; you don't want to arrive and discover everyone is out at the carnival. Each country will also demand documents – birth certificates, passports and evidence of single status (e.g. divorce documents or death certificate of a former spouse) – and the embassy or consulate can help you determine which.

HANDING OVER THE STRESS

There are now many reputable tour organisations that offer wedding packages. They can take care of everything from ceremonies to honeymoons. This is a good option if you are planning to marry somewhere very exotic or with a language you don't understand because they can provide someone with specialist local knowledge who can help out with any problems that might occur.

The tour company can often organise the ceremony and find the celebrant, and even offer wedding cakes, photographer, flowers and champagne. Make sure you check what you're getting, though – the local Chateau de Gastric '89 might not be to your taste. As you often have to be in your chosen location for a few days before the ceremony, you might prefer to make your own arrangements for flowers and decoration – a collection of seashells from the beach and some local blooms, for instance.

Most tour operators ask for photocopies of the required legal documents (e.g. birth certificates) to be sent to them around two months before travelling. The original documents should be carried on the journey.

You need to take care of your skin too when hitting the sun, so check out IDEA 19, *Get glowing.*

Try another idea...

'*Remember that happiness is a way of travel – not a destination.*'
ROY M. GOODMAN

Defining idea...

93

JUST A G-STRING EACH

When choosing what you want to wear, remember that your outfits need to be comfortable and not too hot, so if you're off to Jamaica for a beach wedding, leave the wool morning suit at home, along with the fifteen metres of French Chantilly lace veil. You may favour a slinky, tiny white bikini and cowboy hat, but if you want something more elaborate you need to make sure it travels well. This may have a strong influence on your choice – remember that stuffing fifteen layers of petticoat in a suitcase will cause the kind of damage to the dress that might never bounce back. You should check with your airline if there is somewhere your outfits can be hung; if not, you need to choose something that can sustain a little stress, such as synthetic fabrics, which crush less. You can also get small hand-steamers to take out creases, or book ahead with your hotel for the laundry service to primp and preen your outfits.

Q **My boyfriend and I are going to get married in St Tropez and sent out our invitations ages ago, but so far we've had very few RSVPs. I feel very frustrated that people are taking so long to get back to us. What should I do to stimulate the responses?**

How did it go?

A *It's not a cheap destination, so maybe they are waiting to see if they can afford it before committing. You need to ask yourself what you would do in their shoes and how you can help them make their minds up.*

Q **But we would make the effort for them. So what help should we give?**

A *Even if you would put yourselves out if the roles were reversed, remember that they may have several other family commitments – perhaps other overseas weddings – during the year, all of which chip away at meagre savings. Have you included a list of alternative accommodation for them in the invite and booking details? To give your invitees the best idea of what to expect, give one in each price bracket: sweet B&B, middle range and super luxury hotels. You have to allow for every pocket. And be graceful if they say no.*

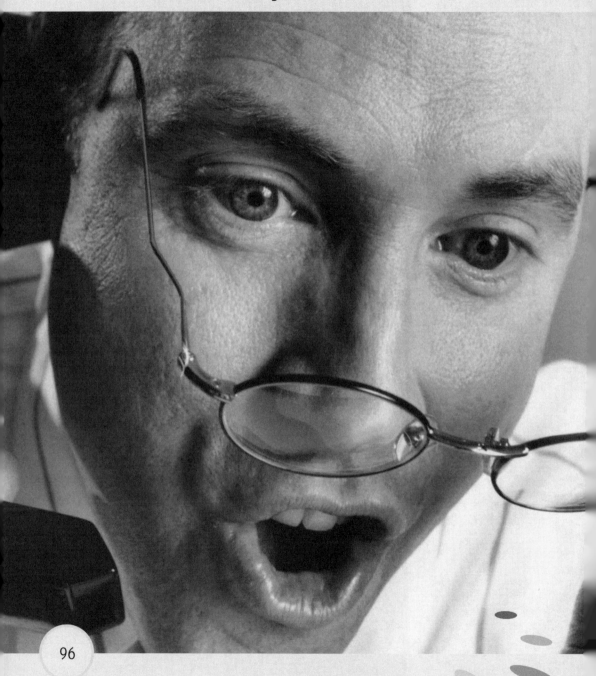

23

Getting your bank manager to say 'I do'

Given that the average UK wedding now costs £15,000, you need to get a handle on your budget, finances and wedding insurance before they get you in a headlock, and find some sneaky ways to save your pennies.

Sensible budgeting will take the stress factor out of the planning, and help you enjoy your big day to the max.

So where does it all go? The honeymoon, reception, and bride's dress amount to approximately half of the total cost. The single biggest expense is usually the honeymoon, with the most popular destinations being the Caribbean and USA. If you are planning something more local, you may have a little more to play with. Just remember that getting yourself into debt will take the edge off your magical day and leave you with a long-term headache that will overshadow your happy memories.

Here's an idea for you... **Early on in your planning, talk to your partner about your priorities. They may see the honeymoon as the big spend, whilst you want top and tails for all the male family members. It's best to consider at the outset what you are happy to compromise on, as budgets can quickly spiral out of control.**

SHOW ME THE MONEY

Although it was traditionally the bride's parents' responsibility, many couples now pay for their own wedding. However, it is also common for the bride and groom's parents and the couple to split the overall bill into thirds. Regardless of how you choose to cover the costs, it is advisable to discuss this with all the parties from the outset; and that includes the deposits that will be required to book everyone from the harpist to the vicar. Losing your dream venue because you are too overdrawn to cover the deposit your future in-laws were meant to pay will not bode well for happy relations.

WHEN DO YOU PAY?

Most of your suppliers will expect a deposit to ensure that the date that you want is secured. You will be expected to pay some of them, such as the band or DJ, the remainder of the balance on the day of the wedding. Make sure the best man has the necessary cash to pay the appropriate people.

MAKING THE MONEY WORK HARDER FOR YOU

Need to make some budget savings? See IDEA 35, *Ways to save*, for a few hints.

Try another idea...

If you have some money saved, make sure you place it in a high interest account so that you are getting a little extra. However, you need to ensure that you can get access to it easily. Do check, because some accounts won't allow immediate withdrawals and these could only work for you if you are super-organised and are planning way ahead and won't need access within the next year or two – but withdraw early and you might have to pay a penalty.

If you need to rely on credit, don't just hand over the old card that has been collecting dust in your wallet since time immemorial. There are lots of great new credit card services that offer interest free deals, so don't be financially lazy, as you could keep your debt interest free if you move your money from card to card every time the interest free offer is up. Just try not to ramp up your borrowing too early on, as you may still have bills rolling in after the big day.

If you are a homeowner, you can also release equity from your mortgage, as it can be a good way of getting a low interest loan to keep your debts in one manageable lump. Your mortgage lender can help you understand the options.

Defining idea...

GETTING SET FOR THE FUTURE

A joint account set up specifically for the arrangements can be a great way of managing the finances relating to your wedding. That way there is no doubt that the spending is fair and controlled, and you can keep up to date with all the expenses. If one of you is a good saver whilst the other is an impetuous spender, make sure that you are both joint signatories. There are different types of account available so shop around for the one that best suits you. Check out overdraft facilities; you will probably need them for a while.

Let your families know that you have set up an account for the wedding, and suggest that they make their contributions to the wedding directly into the account. This will ensure that you don't have to keep harassing them for deposit cheques. If they cannot place a lump sum in the account, perhaps a direct debit that helps cover expenses as they come up is the best way to go.

Q   **I want a nice wedding, but my fiancée is obsessed with staging something grand enough for the royal family. I have tried to explain to her that we can't afford it but she doesn't seem to listen. How can I open her eyes to the reality?**

Try another idea...

A   *You need to get out some pen and paper, and your bank statement. Show how the spending and borrowing will affect your future life. She might not be keen to go from princess to eating beans for breakfast, dinner and tea.*

Q   **Done that; didn't work. She still insists on the spending. What else can I do?**

A   *It sounds like she is suffering from a reality blind spot. In this case, insist that she gets involved in finding a suitable loan or best deal re-mortgage. Once people start to understand money, and its implications on their everyday life, they often get more realistic about it.*

24

Gimme, gimme, gimme

Getting married has some great perks (apart from a lifelong commitment from your soul mate, of course). One of them is the gift list.

Already got two of everything? Or do you want to upgrade to more expensive stuff but can't bring yourself to ask for that Italian glassware? Make your gift list work for you.

Traditionally, guests gave the couple gifts to help them set up home. However, depending on your age, whether you already have your own home or if it's your second wedding, your needs will probably be different.

If you are living together for the first time, then you need to cover all the basics from wooden spoons to linen. Rather than mercenary, gift lists are a good way of making sure that you don't end up with seven toasters and no cutlery. The way to make sure that your list is inclusive is to make sure you include everything from an egg timer right through to a DVD player. Make sure that you know exactly who gave you what, so that you can thank them. It is important that you should be able to tell your Aunt Phyllis when she pops over that you use her teapot every morning (unless she got you a garden swing).

Here's an idea for you... **Commission a special piece of furniture by a local craftsperson. Why not a bedstead, so that your guests can present you with your marital bed?**

You can get things for the house and still be a little adventurous. As it is a given that many couples often have the things that they need, most people are prepared to buy something a little different. You may ask people to make a contribution to a piece of art or a piece of furniture. You can even consider a trip: hot air ballooning or holiday, or even the honeymoon.

But, before you start visualising yourself climbing into your scuba suit, ask yourself if you *really* have everything. After all, couldn't some super-soft, huge waffle bath sheets replace those towels? And what about a full set of china that actually matches? This is an opportunity to select items you would never normally think to splash out on (like a proper dinner service, which can cost hundreds of pounds) that you will be able to enjoy for years to come. And your own kids will probably be more excited to be presented with a cherished family heirloom than a photo album of your diving trip in the Maldives.

Make sure that you do the list together, and go to the relevant department stores to choose things together. This should be one of the fun, relatively stress-free tasks in planning your wedding. And try to give each other a couple of free passes to choose something totally self-indulgent. Take a visit to some of the other departments in the stores; if you really have all the pots and pans you will ever need, what about a leather backgammon set or tennis racquets? (Then you can tell your guests that they bought you your six-pack.) A great investment, and a slightly more elegant approach than asking for cold cash, is to ask for donations towards a cellar of good wine. Guests can ring up and buy wines in multiples of bottles. If you are uncomfortable with asking for specifics, then you could consider using one of the wedding lists that allow you to redeem your gift values in vouchers. (However, you may have to deal with some disappointment from those who would prefer to see their gifts being part of your marital home.)

If you want your guests to travel abroad for your wedding, ask them to make this your wedding gift: see IDEA 22, I married a-broad!

Try another idea...

When choosing a list, you also need to check other details, such as how and when the store can deliver the gifts and if they can exchange unwanted items (or doubles). Make sure that the delivery is after your honeymoon so that your house is not full of unattended gifts. Some lists like to deliver before the wedding but make sure that it all works within your time frame.

SAY PLEASE WITH EASE

The easiest way to let your guests know that you have a wedding list is to include it in your invitations, on a separate card. You must make it clear that people know they can make their own choices of gifts. It might seem a little mercenary, but it is a lot less uncomfortable than making friends call and request the list – and it is now standard practice.

SAYING THANKS

It may seem old fashioned to write thank you cards, but it is essential if you want to make people feel special and appreciated. You may want a design printed that reflects the theme and style of the other wedding stationery.

'*Man's best possession is a sympathetic wife.*'
EURIPIDES

Defining idea...

How did it go?

Q **My aunt wants to buy us an antique for our wedding, as she believes it will hold its value. But our style is very minimal and it just won't go in our flat. Is there a tactful way we can put her off?**

A *I believe that it is wrong to turn down a gift, as the giver should derive just as much pleasure as the receiver. For some, ticking things off a list isn't an expression of their style. Try getting involved with the purchase: ask for a painting or a jewellery box – something that's a manageable size and you can get out when she comes over.*

Q **How rigid should we be with the items specified on our list?**

A *It depends on how much respect you have for your friends' and families' taste. If there are definite items and brands you want, spell it out on the list. There will be some people who will relish the shopping challenge, so it would be nice if you include other present ideas that give them the option of buying something they think you will like.*

25

Drink and be merry

It's an ancient tradition that guests raise a glass of the hard stuff to congratulate the happy couple – these days, it tends to be several. Get your wine right and the party will flow.

If you are having a sit-down meal, you need to provide wine, water and soft drinks. It is also standard to provide champagne for the toast, and often as the guests arrive and are milling around.

When planning your wine order, for a start you need to know that there are six standard 12.5 cl glasses to a bottle. Some people will drink more than a bottle, some less (children under five, perhaps), so when making your calculations base it on one bottle per person. Soft drinks and mineral water should be available for people who have to drive, teetotallers and children. If you want to be especially nice, consider having a special alcohol-free cocktail for the non-drinkers. And if you make it a tasty option, it will also encourage other guests to pace their drinking – no one wants to see your gran start the dancing on her own after a sherry or two too many, especially if there is no music.

Look into having a cocktail made in your honour to serve to the guests on arrival. If you have a colour theme, why not ask a great mixologist at a good local cocktail bar or hotel to create one for you? The same staff might be available for hire themselves, which would give you a bar with real flair.

TO PAY BAR OR NOT TO PAY BAR?

You may begin your planning by intending to pay for all the alcohol at the wedding. However, you could be unpleasantly surprised at how quickly that tots up. Don't worry, though, whatever configuration of free/pay bar you choose, it is pretty standard these days for guests to buy their own drinks after a certain point.

A good way of splitting the responsibilities is to put a set amount behind the bar, which then becomes a pay bar after it runs out. You should, however, make provisions for a welcome drink for all the guests as they arrive at the reception. A nice way to do this is to have waiters with trays of champagne and soft drinks at the room's entrance. This makes it clear that it is a welcome drink, rather than a moveable bar to revisit.

CRUISING FOR A BOOZING

A fun part of the wedding preparations can often be a quick nip across the Channel to top up on the wedding wines. It can save you a great deal of money, although you need to ensure, before you do your sums and spend the savings on shoes, that you check the corkage costs if you are holding your reception at a venue.

This can vary from as little as 50p to a few pounds. Don't be frightened to ask for a special deal – and if you're holding your do at your parents', refuse to pay, point blank! If you have a caterer, check if they have a corkage fee, too. And remember that a licence is needed to sell alcohol in most hired halls and even at home. So you would need to provide all the drinks or apply for a special drinks licence. Get in touch with your local council if you are unsure.

You need to consider the menu as soon as you start thinking about wine. Look at IDEA 28, *Food of love*, so you can plan in tandem.

Try another idea...

If you're using a local vineyard or wine shop, ask if they can offer discounts on bulk orders and if they will take returns of unopened bottles. Let them know you are getting married and ask what they can do; they may offer to lend glasses, supply free ice or recommend a good toastmaster.

GLASS HIRE

Presentation is vital, so you might also want to try glass hire from your local wine shop or supermarket; that way everything will look sharp. Check if there is a supplement for returning dirty glasses; often there isn't, which will make life a lot simpler. Organise a rota of people to serve at the bar if this is not one of the caterer's duties. Most people will be glad to help for a short period.

'From wine what sudden friendship springs.'
JOHN GAY, from *The Squire and His Cur*

Defining idea...

Q **I'm a bit confused about which wine to choose. I don't like red wine but we are having fillet of beef for the main meal. Can we ignore the norms?**

A *Firstly, unless you are drinking all of the wine yourself, it's perfectly acceptable to have both, especially as there will be other white wine lovers and red wine haters in the party. And it's not the colour of the wine that should be the defining element when choosing wine; it's the body and flavour.*

Q **If I can have white wine with red meat, what should I look for?**

A *When choosing wedding wines, go for crowd pleasers: something dependable and drinkable, something that won't give everybody a nasty hangover and is a well-known name that guests are comfortable with. Don't spend too much money as it won't be appreciated. People are looking for something pleasant to quaff, like a quality southern hemisphere (Chilean or Australian) brand. Go for reliable all-rounders, like a good Cabernet Sauvignon and a Chardonnay.*

26

The supporting cast

The wedding party is more than just the two of you, unless you are running away to Gretna Green. You need to work out who you want to do what, and how to get them to do it.

If you are remotely popular, there will be people jostling for the top roles like a rugby scrum in stilettos. Your talents for organisation and diplomacy will have to shine.

Luckily, some of the roles in the wedding day bandwagon are naturally taken care of – like the role of father of the bride (unless your mother was rather too popular herself). If you don't have someone to fill this role, consider another close family member or a special friend, man or woman; their key qualification is that you love each other.

Bridesmaids are usually either a sister of the bride or groom, a close friend of the bride or a niece or nephew. Choose who you want, but remember you can always fall back on this tradition if you need to dissuade an eager friend who keeps hinting heavily. When choosing someone to play these roles, consider that the maid of honour should be someone responsible and willing to help, as you will need

Here's an idea for you... **If you want everyone to pass by the receiving line, you may end up with a glut of people waiting to enter the reception. To make sure that the natives don't get restless, plan to have waiters circulating with welcome drinks and nibbles.**

support and some hen night organising. She can then ask the other bridesmaids awkward questions, like what their hip measurements are, and pressgang them into doing errands – so you can play the good cop, bad cop game. Little ones and ring bearers will not be expected to take an active part in the planning stage but their mothers may get involved instead.

A way for the groom to soothe the egos of those not voted into the best man slot is to appoint them as ushers. (If it seems too hard to pick between choices for the top slot, choose a brother or other male relative.) These positions were normally given to the bride's brothers, but these days anything goes; for a church wedding you will need at least three and make sure one is delegated the job of pampering the close family members. They should hand out orders of ceremony and herd people into the correct pews. They should also be made to oversee any transport arrangements and help band members, speakers and any other 'turns' for the ceremony know their place – physically and in the running order.

Attendants are often flower girls and boys, or ring bearers (although strictly speaking this term also applies to bridesmaids too). They can be nieces, nephews or just children of close family friends. Just make sure that you don't overwork them or expect them to be all that well behaved. They probably don't realise that you are meant to be the star of the show, so if they decide to wander off half way down the aisle in the wrong direction, don't be surprised or annoyed.

Mums have been pivotal in your entire existence, yet the old-fashioned rituals of the wedding feast mean they tend to have little to do. You can always change the rules and let them give a speech, and at the very least you should present them with flowers at the reception in front of your assembled guests, probably just after the speeches.

You'll want to show your appreciation to your special helpers by giving them gifts – **IDEA 27, *Thank yous and gifts*, will tell you who should get what.**

Try another idea…

HELLO!

Another way of making the family and attendants feel special is with the receiving line. It's a great way of making guests feel important and welcomed too; some will have travelled a long way to celebrate with you, and it ensures that they get their chance to chat to you all.

A traditional receiving line includes the bride's mother and father, the groom's mother and father, the bride, and the groom, and it is also quite common for the bride's maid of honour and best man to be there. These days, it is quite common to create a more varied line: many families don't follow the traditional format, so many receiving lines won't either. Approach this with tact: you need to bear in mind that some divorced parents may be remarried while others are still single, so mix them up amongst other celebrants so

'The ritual of marriage is not simply a social event; it is a crossing of threads in the fabric of fate. Many strands bring the couple and their families together and spin their lives into a fabric that is woven on their children.'
Portuguese-Jewish wedding ceremony.

Defining idea…

people don't end up doing a married 'who's who'. You may also want to include brothers, sisters and grandparents – just don't make your list so long that the guests finish the line looking a bit stunned from all the small talk.

How did it go?

Q   What do I do if I know I'm going to upset some friends by not giving them a key role?

A   *There are so many different aspects to arranging your wedding that it's likely you will be able to involve all of your nearest and dearest if you can let them share some parts of your decision-making processes, and perhaps enlist their help. Use a reasoned argument, if needs be – if your aspiring best man lives 200 miles away, point out that you really need a local best friend to get the job done. It's never personal between true friends.*

Q   I have a huge extended family of half brothers and sisters, and really don't want a reception line that is bigger than the rest of the accumulated guests added together. But how do I choose? They would all be seriously offended to be left out.

A   *Forget honesty; sometimes it is far from the best policy. Why not create your own moving reception line? Tell them you are worried about people not knowing each other and mixing, and ask them to circulate amongst the crowd and start to warm things up.*

27

Thank yous and gifts

Much as you feel it should be just your special day, it can't all be one-way traffic. There are a few little nods of gratitude and appreciation you need to make to your nearest and dearest for all their hard work.

You will probably feel that you have said thank you a thousand times during the day, but an elegant couple will write a thank you note for every gift and message received.

PUTTING IT ON PAPER

It makes sense to order your thank you notes along with your other stationery. It's fine to have 'thank you' printed across your cards, and any motifs you included in the other wedding stationery, but you must hand write a personal message yourself. You will need to make them all slightly different: there will be guests who can't make it, who need to be told they were missed; thanks have to go to those who gave you money or vouchers, who need to be told what their contributions will be used for; and there are people who will have given you specific gifts, which need to be acknowledged by name.

Here's an idea for you...

Consider thanking both sets of parents with their own albums of the wedding. These albums could contain a special configuration of prints that focus on them and other family members more than just a replica of yours. Include on the opening page a special thank you note, with the dates and all of your names, plus a special message to show your appreciation.

As a standard guide, thank you notes are sent within two weeks to acknowledge gifts that arrive before the wedding. Although you may feel that you have a lot of other things to consider, it will save you time and spread good will in the long run. Gifts received after or during the ceremony have a longer period of grace to allow for the honeymoon and the couple settling in, but you still need to send them within two months of your wedding day.

When wording the card, mention the giver by name and the gift that you received. Tell them why you like it and how useful it will be. Don't be too stiff, even if you had a really formal wedding. Be chatty and warm, and, if you can, include a personal memory of them on the day or a picture of them at the wedding. Try splitting the task: get a bottle of wine on a Friday night and try to work through them together. Also, don't automatically say 'we' as it adds to the formal theme – you could always write half the note each. Another approach would be to try writing a few letters each evening for as long as you can keep your enthusiasm fresh and perky. Make sure you don't feel resentful as you write them; it will show in the tone and feel you give the notes.

SPECIAL THANK YOUS FOR SPECIAL PEOPLE

The groom has on his list of responsibilities gifts for the bridesmaids, attendants, ushers and the best man. These don't have to be extravagant but do need to be serious rather than flippant to show your appreciation. Consider necklaces or bracelets for the bridesmaids. You may want to give such gifts out on the morning of the ceremony so that they can wear them on the day and forever associate them with your marriage. You should consider getting the chief bridesmaid a slightly more elaborate gift, or a larger version, for all her extra efforts.

For flower girls and ring bearing boys, you should expect disappointment, but it probably means you have chosen something with appropriate *gravitas*. Your four-year-old niece might not seem very excited about a silver locket that isn't (a) pink or (b) plastic, but her parents will appreciate it, and so will she in later years.

As for the ushers, consider something matching to keep, like cufflinks or silk ties that they can use again. For the best man, as for the chief bridesmaid, give something with a little edge over the others, such as a leather wallet or gold tie pin. You could even have your gifts engraved to remind them of your special day. If they aren't the type to appreciate a sartorial gesture, picture frames with a snap of you all in your finery might be a nice idea; after all, you may never see it again.

Try another idea...

Choosing your stationery? Take a look at IDEA 34, *Start spreading the news*, on what you'll need.

Defining idea...

'If the only prayer you ever say in your whole life is "thank you", that would suffice.'
MEISTER ECKHART

How did it go?

Q Complete horror! I've just found a new stack of cards from wedding gifts that I haven't replied to, from my wedding six months ago! Can I ever make amends?

A *Of course you can. Get out your address book and start writing. It is not uncommon for couples to send out thank you cards in waves, as there are so many to send out. Something pleasant, that isn't in a bill format, hitting the doormat usually erodes any bad feeling immediately on contact.*

Q But isn't six months a rather excessive delay?

A *Just don't try to hide from the truth – give a reason for the delay and explain how mortified you feel. Emphasise that the gift was appreciated just as much as all the others that you received.*

28

Food of love

You might be too happy to eat, but your guests will certainly expect a little nourishment. But will a sit-down meal for 200 or a ham sandwich in your local fit the bill?

The format of the meal will greatly influence your menu. Your choice is almost limitless if you choose a formal meal, but bear in mind that large numbers will require dishes that can also be made comfortably en masse — so, no soufflé for 300. Three courses are usually standard.

To begin with, you need to decide what part food will be playing in your festivities, and then make a decision about how that will be achieved. If you would like a proper feast, your options are formal sit-down meal or buffet. The first will require waiter service; a formal buffet will, too, since it will be eaten with knives and forks, sitting at proper tables, and therefore need to be cleared afterwards. Another idea is

'I only eat reindeer.' Of course, some of your guests will have special dietary requirements, and they need to be catered for. There are a variety of food foibles these days, so just having a vegetarian option won't cut it. Find out if any of your guests are gluten intolerant, have seafood allergies or must avoid certain dishes on religious grounds. Always make sure you have a few extra portions of the vegetarian options; someone is almost guaranteed to have forgotten to make their needs known on their RSVP.

the more casual finger buffet, which is eaten whilst standing and will not need to be cleared away immediately. Obviously, for weddings held at home, the last is the most suitable option, unless you are planning a marquee.

A sit-down buffet will allow you to plan the seating arrangements, but is a slightly more affordable (and often less stressful) option than the banquet. It used to be a collection of cold foods, but now they often include hot dishes too. A finger buffet allows people to eat and mingle, and is often a great choice when you are pressed for time or squeezed by your budget. Remember, though, that you still need to provide some chairs for children, pregnant ladies and the elderly. (You should make provisions for these people throughout the day whatever format you decide on.)

Canapés are an elegant way to look after your guests as they await the formal sit-down dinner, and also as a means of ensuring that evening guests are catered for. Your caterer should be able to offer you a selection of options, so plan a tasting session and see what you like. Ask to see photographs of previous events, as presentation is essential.

HIRING CATERERS

If you plan to use the catering services of the venue you have hired – hotel or restaurant – try them out before confirming. That way you can see their approach. (Extra staff may be hired in on the day for your wedding, but at

Thinking of doing it yourself? Ease the burden by considering the easiest way to handle the liquid part of the refreshments: see IDEA 25, *Drink and be merry*, for some options that will help you out.

Try another idea...

least it gives you a feel for things.) If the food is dreadful under normal service conditions, you are unlikely to get a good standard when the kitchen has to cope with a hundred covers at once.

For outside catering companies, seek recommendations from everyone you know. Eaten fabulously at a friend's wedding? Ask for the number. Great canapés at the work Christmas party? Find out who organised it and raid their address book. A reputable caterer should also be able to give you references.

Caterers (and hotels) will also have sample menus that cover different price ranges. They are a great place to get inspiration: ask if you can mix and match from their sample menus, and don't be afraid to make special requests. Do remember, though, that the dishes will need to be made in hefty quantities within a strict time frame, so be reasonable.

Look at the venue's recommended caterers; they will know the layout of the kitchens and therefore should be able to make things run smoothly. If the venue is new to the caterers, they should carry out a site visit to ensure that they have all they need to prepare the menu you have planned.

Defining
idea...

**'A good cook is like a
sorceress who dispenses
happiness.'**
ELSA SCHIAPIRELLI, French fashion
designer

For a marquee, they will need to bring all of their own equipment, such as ovens, and be able to handle all of the disposal and clearing of waste and bottles. Make sure that you know what you are both responsible for. Make sure that they have a head waiter who can act as intermediary between your best man and the kitchen so that the cutting of the cake, champagne toast and clearing are all done efficiently. You may even want to give them a copy of the schedule. Many of us have been to a wedding that is so delayed that everyone is too tipsy to take any interest in the starter that arrives two hours late.

Ask your caterers what extras they can provide: can they organise extra staff to do the coat check and run the bar after the meal is over? They also will have contacts for chairs and tables, cutlery and linen, so ask, but you needn't stick with their suppliers.

Q **We're having a budget crisis, and need to cut back drastically somewhere. The obvious choice is the buffet at the evening reception, but I feel it's mean to have guests travel – some from a long way – and not cater fully for them. Will they think us terribly unwelcoming if we do?**

How did it go?

A *If you've not stated that you'll be serving food at the reception on your invitations, then anything you provide will be an added bonus. Why don't you consider a compromise by providing substantial canapés and roping in some keen younger cousins as your waiting staff?*

Q **In the early planning stages, how can we keep some flexibility in the catering costs of our evening bash?**

A *Your caterers should be able to provide you with something special on a budget so ask them for ideas. If you are doing the food yourself, make sure you choose something that can be made well in advance and stored easily. Consider employing someone to do the heating and final preparation on the night – after all, you can't expect your mum or friends to spend hours in the kitchen when they should be enjoying themselves.*

123

29

Be the best guest going

There are many stories of guests from hell, falling from grace as they collapse over the top table onto the bride's mother. Oh, how we laughed. The bride and groom didn't, though.

The wedding day belongs to the bride and groom and all of the guests should remember that. The warmth of their support and love will make sure the couple's enjoyment of their big day is complete.

The best way to start accruing good guest points, is to RSVP promptly. The couple will have a lot to think about already, and as a lot of decisions they need to finalise will be based on numbers, it is very impolite to leave them hanging.

WISHING THEM WELL WITH A BIG BOW ON IT

When choosing a gift, make sure you choose them something from the list. You may feel it is a bit impersonal, but at least you know you will be getting something

Here's an idea for you...

When it comes to alcohol, be mindful of your limits. It is entirely inappropriate to get drunk during the meal and heckle during the toasts. A lot of hard work, thought and consideration has gone into these speeches, so resist your witty asides. You must pace your intake. Drinking during the meal, the toasts, all often before six o'clock? Make sure that every other drink is a soft drink, as it will help you stay perky and also make the next day easier by keeping your hangover to a minimum.

they really need and like. It is very easy to give them something you like, that you *think* they should like. However, it's very possible that they will hate it and be too polite to say. So stick with the plan unless you know them very well and could stake your life on the premise that they will love your surprise.

Weddings are becoming increasingly expensive, so you can factor that in when choosing your gift; don't feel pressured to choose something you can't afford just because the list they have put together is very expensive. If the gifts in your price range have gone from the list, why not try and partner up with some friends to buy a bigger gift? Don't get it monogrammed unless you know that they are certain to keep it, as they won't be able to exchange it. When buying from the list ask for gift wrapping and delivery so that you don't have to take it to the wedding.

Any questions that you have, if possible, should be addressed to the bridesmaids or best man, so that you don't inundate the probably not-so-happy, stressed-out couple. As a rule, don't assume that you can take children unless they are specifically listed on the invitation. If you do take them, make sure provision is made for children during the evening – unruly, overtired nippers are almost never welcome.

Stick to the dress code that has been stated. If you are unsure, dress up. It's better that you make too much effort than not enough.

Not sure what to get them? Check out IDEA 24, *Gimme, gimme, gimme*, for some unusual suggestions.

Try another idea...

If you are invited to the ceremony, make sure you are there with at least fifteen minutes to spare; the only big entrance should be made by the bride. If you are unsure of the proper place to sit, see the ushers. If there is a receiving line at the reception, make sure that you don't hog the wedding party – you may be bursting with joy and a monologue of only a thousand words that you prepared earlier, but they have a lot of people to say hello to. By the same token, don't be offended if you only manage to see the back of their heads most of the time, as they will be very busy.

Wait for the bride and groom to hit the dance floor before you do. Do *not* do a dramatic slide across the floor and try and knock them down like dominoes – no one besides you will think it's funny. This is meant to be a treasured moment, so try and act with some decorum.

Bear in mind that this is also meant to be a celebration with a purpose; a celebration of two people and their families coming together. The best guests show consideration to the other people around them. Make sure that you mix, and talk to your neighbours at sit-down meals. Include any single guests in your party and make sure you seek out key family members, like parents and grandparents; it's a special day for them too.

'*True friends are those who really know you but love you anyway.*'
EDNA BUCHANAN, novelist

Defining idea...

127

How did
it go?

Q **I'm a single woman and I've been invited to a friend's wedding. But I'm told I can't bring anybody with me. I feel so annoyed because my friends in couples are allowed to take their partners, so why should I be penalised?**

A *I can appreciate your feelings, but the main problem with weddings tends to be money, and extra guests equal extra money. You'll have to try not to take this personally and focus on the happiness of the bride and groom.*

Q **I appreciate that but I don't want to go alone. Can I ask them about this?**

A *You could quietly request that they give you the opportunity to bring a guest, if they have room, once they've received all their RSVPs. If they still say no, you need to consider whether or not you would be able to go and enjoy it, or if you should bow out gracefully and just send them a gift. There's no point in going if you will feel uncomfortable all day.*

30

Honeymoon

The stuff of Blackpool postcards, but that doesn't make it your dream destination. You need to plan carefully if you are hoping to find your ideal blissful bolthole, with guaranteed sun (or snow).

Just so you know, it is traditionally the responsibility of the groom to plan the honeymoon. However, times change and the bride often wants equal involvement.

So what exactly does 'honeymoon' mean? It originates from the times when a man captured his bride and they would hide from the bride's parents before marrying. They would remain in hiding for a further cycle of the *moon* after the wedding. During this period they drank *honey* wine.

You will probably need a break after the wedding to recover from all the stress and chaos of the run up to the big day. In which case, plan the honeymoon carefully and make sure you splash out on a few extras like cars to meet and transport you, and nice comfy airline seats. Tell everyone that you are honeymooners because you will often get free upgrades with rooms and flights if they are available, and nice touches from the hotels, such as complimentary champagne in the room.

Ask your friends and relatives about their honeymoons. As well as some great ideas for your holiday, you might get an idea of some places to avoid (not to mention a few great stories for the speeches).

You can always choose one of the specialist packages on offer. Most companies have a specific brochure that relates to honeymoons, but different companies may offer the same hotels with different rates and packages so make sure you shop around before settling. If you are using a travel agent, make sure that they present you with some options and earn their commission; don't just always settle for the first option that they come up with. Some hotels often insist that you produce your marriage certificate to qualify for special treatment, so don't forget to take it.

If you are booking directly, make sure you are very clear about what is included. The images you will be shown do not necessarily reflect your room, so ask if you will get a room of a comparable standard. Don't take anything for granted, such as a sea view, as you need to get written confirmation from the hotel about what you will be offered.

WHERE TO?

Make sure you have a serious think about all the honeymoon options. You don't have to go with the traditional destinations in the brochures. It may be sold as the fantasy of every new honeymooner, but if you are usually rock climbing or clubbing at the weekend, is being marooned on a sleepy island really right for you? It can be huge pressure for you to go from busy working lives to suddenly staring at each other every day across cocktails in coconuts. If you do choose a resort holiday, make sure you take time off from each other with the odd spa treatment or round of golf, so you can look forward to seeing each other again.

If you have ever wanted to take a longer break, many companies offer the option of a lengthier getaway than your usual two-week allowance. You could always use this as a chance to visit the rainforest in Brazil or go whale watching in the North Pole.

When planning to leave your reception, make sure you do it in style. See IDEA 16, *Make an entrance*, to make sure you get yourself a suitable carriage.

Try another idea...

MAKING IT STRESS FREE

When planning your honeymoon, consider the location of your wedding and the reception. You might like the idea of jetting off straight away, but a four-hour car journey to the airport can take the edge off your exciting day. Consider booking a special hotel nearby so that you can still leave the reception, but don't have to turn up in a flustered state. Have your suitcases delivered to your wedding suite in the morning so you don't have to think about it as the honeymoon begins. Make sure it's a special suite, and a pretty location. You might not see much of the grounds or spa on this visit, but you might want to return there for your anniversary.

Practically speaking, you need to make sure that you have all you need before heading off. Some more exotic locations may require special jabs and documentation, so ensure that you have this covered before you hit the airport. As soon as you have chosen a destination, get a list of required vaccinations and make sure you have time to get them done; you might need to take a course, or have them spaced out, so allow enough time.

'Only passions, great passions, can elevate the soul to great things.'
DENIS DIDEROT, French philosopher

Defining idea...

How did it go?

Q   I'm already stressed out and the wedding's months off. I really want some time off to look forward to on the honeymoon, but my spouse to be – who, I have to say, has managed to duck all of the hassles – wants to do something adventurous. What can I do?

A   Be clear and tell your partner how you feel. Then there are three ways of getting round this. First, you could choose a location that offers activities as well as a great pool or beach to lounge around. That way you can slob out until you have recovered and then join him in the more active pursuits. Second, you can try a twin-centre holiday, where you visit a beach location like the Seychelles, and then try taking a short hop over to Kenya for a safari.

Q   And the third option?

A   Separate honeymoons.

31
Let them eat cake

Most women regard themselves as experts when it comes to cake, but there is a bit more to this one than meets the eye. It is as important to foodies as the dress, and usually takes centre stage at the reception. So you need to get it right.

The ritual of cutting the cake is also a key part of the marriage: the couple's joint first slice into it symbolises their shared future. Announced by the toastmaster, this usually happens after the speeches.

Wedding cakes have had all kinds of formats and recipes over the years, but the modern shape, with three tiers of iced cake, was believed to have been inspired by Saint Bride's Church in London. Tradition has it that bridesmaids who sleep with a piece under their pillow will dream of their future husbands (and wake up with cake in their hair, and possibly having their faces licked by the family pet). The top tier of the cake is often kept by couples for the christening of their first child.

Here's an idea for you... **Half and half? If your gran is adamant that her family cake will grace your reception table, but she is a little out of touch with contemporary decoration, get it finished by a professional. Alternatively, if you don't want the stress of making it taste good but want the chance to make it look pretty, get it baked elsewhere and do the fun stuff yourself (as long as you do so well in advance).**

Traditionally, it is a fruitcake with royal icing decoration, but many couples don't adhere to this nowadays – it is perfectly common to have a sponge cake, or a tower of profiteroles, and even a cheesecake. (Honestly!) It really is a matter of preference, but if you want to carry on with some of the classic cake traditions, such as the saving of the top layer for new arrivals and sending some to absent guests, it needs to keep and travel; bear this in mind when you order the cake. You need to add this factor to the calculations of the appropriate size of cake for the number of guests.

CHOOSING THE STYLE AND DECORATION

Symbols that often graced wedding cakes traditionally include horseshoes and tiny models of brides and grooms. These days though, your only limitation is your imagination. Consider incorporating fresh flowers, exotic colours or graphic shapes. Why not have your names spelled out in letters or a stack of fairy cakes replicating a traditional wedding cake silhouette? Stock up on heaps of wedding magazines and gorge yourself on the styles and variety available. Make sure you rip them out and keep them in a file, but try not to include every single one that you see. If you choose your own pastry chef, they will have a portfolio that will show their previous commissions and styles. These should only be guidelines, though, which they should be happy to tailor in terms of size and style to fit your wishes, number of guests and budget.

FINDING A PASTRY CHEF

Wedding fairs are a great place to find a
suitable pastry chef, and they also give you the
chance to munch cake legitimately while you
wander around looking at wedding portfolios.
(It's all in the name of research, you understand.) If you are having the catering
provided by a professional outside company or hotel, they may also be able to
supply the wedding cake or have a contact who can.

When you have found a pastry chef that you like, you should be able to enjoy a
tasting with them. Once again, this is in the interest of the greater good. Tell them
what your concerns are, your requirements and budget. The wedding cake should
be ordered at least three months in advance. The cake is usually delivered to the
venue on the morning of the reception, where they should add any final touches in
situ. When it comes to the cutting of the cake, make sure that you have organised
with your caterers if you want them to cut the cake for guests. You need to let them
know how many pieces you need (including
the absent guests) and if you want to keep the
top layer uncut. Your pastry chef should also be
able to tell you about the proper way to store
this cake for future use.

**Make sure that your cake suits
your theme or picks up the
motifs of your flowers: see
IDEA 12, *The bouquets*, on
selecting blooms to decorate.**

Try
another
idea...

*'Qu'ils mangent de la
brioche.' [Let them eat cake.]*
MARIE ANTOINETTE

Defining
idea...

MAKING YOUR OWN

In spite of it being considered as bringing bad luck, it is not a completely crazy notion that you could make your own cake. However, if you are well known as a disaster area in the kitchen, it probably would be crazy. If you do decide to bake the cake yourself, then you need to plan to make it at least a month before the wedding. This gives you plenty of time to tick it off your list before the day draws near. You can hire any necessary equipment, like outsize cake tins, from events companies and specialist cookery shops.

How did
it go?

Q   **I love the idea of having a traditional cake, but my partner's family are strict vegetarians and they've given me a huge list of things that can't be included in the recipe! Can I keep all of us happy?**

A   *Don't panic, there are lots of substitutes for traditional ingredients these days. Try having a look through a couple of veggie cookery books to get some ideas.*

Q   **How about accommodating people with intolerance to specific foods?**

A   *It can be done. However, if you really feel like it will spoil your plans, then why not make a separate cake for them? You can always make a point of asking the other guests with food intolerances to state any specific needs and then you can handle them and the vegetarians all in one go.*

32
Keeping hangovers at bay

Even the most abstemious of us may get a little tipsy in the face of a happy union and end up being distinctly foggy the next day. However, you can easily help yourself and your guests avoid the worst.

Prevention is without doubt the best cure for hangovers. With commonsense regulation of what you all eat and drink you'll minimise those 'morning after the night before' feelings.

The first major weapon on the front line in the battle against hangovers is good old H_2O. Dehydration is a major factor so make sure that there is a free and plentiful supply of water for all your guests. Another key strategy in avoiding a hangover (mainly that horrible uncomfortable acidic stomach) is eating. Starchy food is best, such as bread and pasta, which will absorb the alcohol. You can't ensure that everyone arriving at your reception is going to have followed this rule, but you can help them by arranging for canapés to be circulated.

You can also make sure that your cocktails are not super alcoholic – make them long drinks, with plenty of mixers and lots of lovely clinking ice (freeze lemon rind inside for extra effect). Make sure that they actually taste like grown-up alcoholic

Here's an idea for you... **Are you from the kill-or-cure school? Some people believe in taking their medicine and getting back under the duvet to watch some no-brainer kids' TV. Others think that exercise will restore well-being – pushing the toxins out of your pores will help, as will taking in extra oxygen, to eliminate the rubbish swilling around in your blood. Whatever your preference, allow your body some down-time while your remedies kick in.**

drinks, if that's what they are – if you don't want to see your mum face down in the flowers on the top table by half six, don't try to disguise the flavour of killer drinks with fruit juice.

Elderflower cordial is the classic soft drink for English weddings, and when mixed with sparkling water is so delicious it's a great alternative to champagne, so have lots on hand. You can also rein in the pain by making sure that you serve a truly decent wine. If you want to pay for all the drinks yourselves but are worried about the budget, remember that no one will appreciate the gesture if any spilled wine strips the varnish off tabletops. They would probably prefer to have a pay bar and miss out on the pain that follows every free glass.

Inform your bar staff to have glasses of water on trays so people can grab them – they might not consider ordering one but are likely to pick it up if it's there. Your guests will thank you in the morning.

You might feel that you are treating your guests like children, but weddings can be like starting a heavy-duty Saturday evening out at nine in the morning. This is not something most people are used to dealing with, so things are bound to be a little harder to control.

THE DAMAGE IS DONE

Oh-oh. It came, it saw you to the floor, it conquered your head. So, what now? Most of the symptoms you'll be experiencing are down to dehydration; not impossible to believe when you consider that we are made up mainly of water. Then there are the toxins in booze – they'll be where your headache's coming from. These leach essentials from your system. The hangover treatments you can pick up from chemist's are full of vitamins to help your depleted reserves.

Considering a main effect of dehydration is losing the ability to think, you should try to follow these simple steps. Drink plenty of water before bed, with some orange juice if possible (waking up in the middle of the night in a panic is due to a sugar crash and dehydration; the orange juice will stop that happening). As soon as you awake, force some water down, and then some more.

The following day, do you need to keep going, catch a flight, or are you just worried about guests travelling home? Make sure you have coffee on hand and, better still, encourage even more water intake. Although coffee and tea may make you feel more perky, they add to the dehydration (which is why coffee shouldn't be used to sober people up).

You might not fancy fruit; you may be yearning for a full-blown fry up instead. However, all those good vitamins are badly needed, and they will be easy for an upset stomach to process.

Thinking about the best way to cause that hangover in the first place? Take a look at IDEA 25, *Drink and be merry*, on how to get the mix right.

Try another idea...

'*Let us have wine and women, mirth and laughter, sermons and soda water the day after.*'
LORD BYRON, from *Don Juan*

Defining idea...

139

How did it go?

Q **I want everyone to enjoy a drink at my wedding, but I don't want people getting drunk. How can I control the situation?**

A *By controlling the flow of alcohol, although I can't imagine why you want to rein them all in. If you try and limit their consumption too much, they may think you're being stingy or a control-freak. The best way to handle it is probably control the flow in the day and then resign yourself to the fact that your guests are adults for the evening.*

Q **I think drunkenness is undignified and I don't want a wedding video of people with ties on their head doing air guitar. What's the best way to manage the flow of alcohol?**

A *Well, weddings tend to be a time for people to let go, so you may have to be prepared to loosen up a little. On a practical level, you can have waiters circulating in the evening with soft drinks and gentle cocktails. Instruct them to take their time between topping up people's glasses (the same rules applying for a sit-down meal) and fill up the water glasses more frequently. If you have a pay bar, there is little you can do realistically – and bear in mind that people will have their own ideas about how much they can, or want to, imbibe. It's a good idea to have the wedding video shot early if you're that worried.*

33

And to your left...

Who sits on the top table; should couples sit together; should you engage in a little subtle matchmaking with the singles table? Seating plans are surprisingly tricky and important.

Mix the right people together and you have a recipe for an unbeatable atmosphere at your reception. Putting ample effort into working out that mix is a must.

When it comes to planning your seating, you should allow at least five years, maybe six. Only joking – the point is, though, seating plans will definitely take up more of your time than you ever thought possible. You will need to employ a lot of subtlety and grace to get it right. A great seating plan will have strangers laughing along together and boosting the general feeling of joy and good cheer. A bad seating plan will lower the temperature in the marquee by about fifty degrees and see tumbleweed rattling between the tables.

Here's an idea for you... **Want your wedding feast to run as smoothly as a five-star restaurant's VIP room? Then ensure that you brief your caterer properly, with a full copy of the seating plan. Clearly mark all the vegetarian/special requirements on it, so that waiting staff don't have to constantly ask. It will make those guests feel extra appreciated.**

With a finger buffet, you can definitely avoid this stress, but any kind of formal meal should have a proper plan. When deciding where to place guests, remember that, rather than a college reunion, this is meant to be the joining of two sets of families and friends, so mix people up. There will be plenty of time for old friends to hook up later in the evening. If something terrible happens, and guests don't arrive for whatever reason, you will still be liable for the cost of the food but, more importantly, you should quickly re-arrange the tables to stop any gaps from becoming apparent.

Special consideration needs to be given to guests who are single or unaccompanied. Don't corral them all on one table – you may as well cover it in snow and flag it 'social Siberia'. The same goes for guests of different ages. It is common to seat children together but you shouldn't put all of your elderly relatives on one table. Be considerate. Although you shouldn't start pimping your single guests, it is a well-known fact that many couples meet at weddings so don't be scared of indulging in some gentle matchmaking.

Little people also need some special thought. A table for small children is a great way of keeping the mess and chaos to a minimum, but really little ones will need to be sat with their parents so make sure provision is made for them. Take into account that children are not known for their patience, so placid, thoughtful consideration during the speeches is probably out. Put them somewhere they can cause a little bit of trouble (like doing headstands on the dance floor) without disrupting the proceedings too much.

While they are waiting to be seated, keep your guests happy with a special tipple. See IDEA 25, *Drink and be merry*, for ideas.

Try another idea...

ROUND OR SQUARE?

Or even one big u-shape, to avoid favouritism. Whatever you go for, just make sure that your tables have a good mix of guests on them; people who, ideally, are comfortable talking to more than just their immediate neighbours. You may find, however, that your table shapes and sizes are dictated by the space and shape of your location. Remember that waiting staff and guests will need to be able to move freely, and the bride will also need to be able to circulate and mingle. Traditionally, most top tables (where the wedding party sits) are rectangular and face the guests, but you can have a round table if you would like to be less formal (or conspicuous, you shy brides).

The basic running order of the top table goes like this: maid of honour, groom's father, bride's mother, bridegroom, bride, bride's father, groom's mother, best man. Of course, you may have step-parents, siblings, ushers and bridesmaids you want to include too. If so, just make sure that the members of the different families are mixed up and have the opportunity to get to know each other better.

'Food is our common ground, a universal experience.'
JAMES BEARD, US chef

Defining idea...

Of course, there is a limit to how many can head up the top table. It is usual for the partners of those on the top table, such as the

143

bridesmaids and best man, to sit together on a table nearby. However, if there are tensions about top table honours, why not break with tradition and have special party members host the tables? They can also take on the important task of getting everyone chatting and at ease.

SIT DOWN!

As guests enter the venue, it is a good idea to have a table plan displayed; even better, two: one on either side of the entrance. This will allow guests to find their places easily and without causing a glut of bumping bodies in the doorway and around the tables. You can use all kinds of methods to differentiate the tables: numbers, vases of different flowers, coloured balloons or ribbons, even naming them after different family pets.

How did it go?

Q   When we're designing our seating plan should we have couples sitting together or apart?

A   If you want your guests to integrate, you should sit them on the same table but apart; maybe opposite each other.

Q   What if there are guests who are shy? My sister couldn't be less gregarious and won't talk to anyone if I sit her away from my brother-in-law.

A   Then it's probably best not to torture her; sit them together. It's a celebration, not an endurance test.

34

Start spreading the news...

You've met the person you want to be with for ever, proposed and, hooray, they feel the same way too. All you need to do now is tell the world. There are quite a few details worth thinking about to get the ball rolling.

Start as you mean to go on — the way you announce your engagement is a great way to set the tone for your whole wedding. And why not have a big party while you're at it?

It is not unusual for brides to choose their own wedding and engagement rings these days, especially as they will be wearing them together. If you want to present your partner with something when you propose (bearing in mind that lots of thoroughly modern women do the asking nowadays), you could present them with a keepsake to mark the occasion, and then pick the rings together. A piece of jewellery such as a necklace or watch might be appropriate and something they could still show off. If you want to present a ring, a nice piece of costume jewellery could be a pretty and memorable stand in. Alternatively, the way you pop the question could be that special something to tide them over until they get their sparkler. Consider taking them to a favourite spot, filling a room with flowers, or

Here's an idea for you...

Get the key elements in place before you get onto the fluffy, enjoyable stuff. Start with date and location for your wedding (which will be the hardest to secure), then your reception venue or marquee hire.

having your proposal grace the notice board at a football stadium. Whatever you do, make it good – this is the story you'll be telling your kids in years to come. A drunken 'Shall we get it over and done with, then?' takes the edge off the romance somewhat.

HOLD THE FRONT PAGE

Are you retiring types who would happily let the news spread by word of mouth, or are you planning a banner trailing behind a plane? An announcement in a national or local newspaper is a popular way of spreading the news. Bear in mind, though, that you pay by the word so this is not the time to write lengthy and profound statements of love (unless money is no object). If you are unsure of the wording, take a look at their announcements page or ask if they have a formal style that you can use.

A whole glut of information is out there waiting for you to find it. There are lots of great web sites to use for ideas. You should also get yourself a big pile of wedding magazines. Try a range of different ones at first to give you a flavour of which ones suit you best. Even if you already know exactly what you want, the web and magazines are a great resource to show you where to find it. And your ideas might need a little overhaul – lots of women last seriously planned their own weddings when they were 12. That replica Princess Diana puff sleeve number that you dreamed of might not look so very 'now' anymore. The same can be said of cakes, dresses and shoes.

Wedding fairs are also hugely useful. These are usually held at a local hotel or popular wedding venue, and are a great way of getting to see local talent in action. Harpists, string quartets, pastry chefs, photographers and florists are among the service providers present at these events. Although you should always look around, a company's regular presence is often a good sign – it shows they are obviously organised and motivated, qualities you will come to appreciate as you undertake a project as time-consuming and stressful (and fun!) as planning a wedding.

Can't decide on where to have your wedding and the reception? IDEA 17, *Where: choosing a location*, will give you lots of ideas on how to select the perfect places.

Try another idea...

'SAVE THE DATE' CARDS

A great way to ensure that you have all your special people with you on your big day is by sending out 'save the date' cards. You don't need to have planned anything further than who you're marrying, and when, to issue these: people's summer weekends can quickly become booked up, so you will certainly want to make sure your wedding goes into their diaries first. These cards can be bought from most stationer's, or you can order them from a printer in the same style that you want for your invitations. If the wedding is to be intimate, you can always rely on a less formal phone call or email.

'Happiness isn't something you experience; it's something you remember.'
OSCAR LEVANT

Defining idea...

Q   We want to have a huge engagement party and really raise the roof, but does that mean we will have to invite everyone who will be coming to the wedding?

A   *Of course not. Many older relatives certainly wouldn't mind missing a boozy night shaking their booties to thumping hip-hop. On the other side of the coin, it's often a great way to include all your pals in the celebrations if you are thinking of having a small wedding or going away.*

Q   And can we ask for specific engagement presents?

A   *Certainly not; it's not appropriate at all. In fact you should accept anything and nothing with the same grace. Just be glad they turn up to wish you well.*

35

Ways to save

One thing that often stays with a couple long after their first anniversary is the overdraft. However, there is no reason for getting yourself hitched to a massive debt when you get hitched. You don't need to compromise on style just because you need to compromise on cost.

No matter how hard you try, things can often seem to spiral out of control. But there are things that you can do to get yourselves back on track. You need to get money savvy.

If you have to borrow money to finance your wedding, get reading the financial pages in the Sunday newspapers and make sure you get the best deals. (It might seem daunting at first but you will soon get the gist of it all.) You can use interest free credit card deals, release equity from your mortgage or get a low interest loan. Make sure your decisions are informed, and don't just go to your bank – they won't always be offering the best rates. By making good choices from the start, you can save yourself a lot of stress and money later.

Here's an idea for you... **Look into taking out wedding insurance to help ease the fear that goes with splashing out so much money in advance. But remember, too, that any suppliers you book should also have their own liability insurance. If a photographer with a technical hitch ruins all your photographs, you want to know that there will be some way to claw the costs back. And although no one likes to think about the worst, you should always ask about the supplier's cancellation policy.**

Check the business hours of your suppliers: sometimes the cost of out-of-hours delivery can really push up your bill. You may even be able to save a small fortune by taking over the collections and deliveries yourself – or, rather, getting a willing helper to take them on. Bear in mind that some things might also have to be returned.

THE GREEN STUFF

Flowers are a prime area for saving. Start by thinking about your venue: does it seem huge and yawning? Do you imagine that it would take Kew Gardens to fill it? If so, try some clever tricks with the lighting. Spots of candlelight can create an intimate glow on tables, and push cavernous high ceilings out of focus.

If another couple will be marrying on the same day as you, save money and time by sharing the cost of ceremony flowers and aisle pew displays. (Some churches include these anyway as part of the service.) Aisle pews don't always need to be decorated, or perhaps you can tackle every second one, alternating with ribbon. When choosing the flowers, make sure they are in season, as they will be much cheaper. If you really want some more exotic blooms, limit them to your bouquet and altar

flowers, and give the displays more body and presence with less expensive blooms in the same shade. Vivid, large displays of greenery or hired trees can be used with – or instead of – flowers to great effect.

Flowers also travel, so if you are having a civil ceremony in a hotel, take the flowers from your altar display through to the reception for the top table. Ensure your florist doesn't bamboozle you with different styles and unnecessary arrangements. You can even try your hand at some aspects yourself, such as the buttonholes: a lovely, simple rose with a little greenery is more than enough for most men and looks very refined and elegant. However, unless you are carrying a single stem, don't attempt anything vital like your own bouquet, as you will be horrified if it goes wrong. And even the most simple country garden bouquet usually has a lot more complexities and scaffolding than us mere mortals will ever understand. Ask the florist about money-saving tricks. For instance, mirrors under a display reflect the flowers and make them seem more bountiful; petals scattered over a white tablecloth look lush and pretty; and one big rose head can cover a standard table easily.

Take a look at IDEA 2, *When: date and time*, for choosing a time of day to make your styling even more cost-effective.

Try another idea...

'Honeymoon: a short period of doting between dating and debting.'
RAY BANDY

Defining idea...

WELL FED

Savings can also be made by making some of the food yourself. If you are having a reasonably small wedding, you should be able to enlist some willing helpers and produce something special between you. The easiest option is a finger buffet, but you can easily make a sit-down meal, too, if you choose your menu wisely – stews and barbeques can be made in large quantities without compromising on taste or quality, and they can all be prepared in advance. You should make sure that some of your food can be frozen so that it can be made a week or two before rather than the day before or you will find yourself too stressed out. Catering equipment, like a very large electric barbeque, outsized pots and pans and refrigerators for the wine, can all be hired. You must have one person in charge on the day, though. Do not make this your mum or another close member of the wedding party, as they won't thank you for missing out on the enjoyment of the day. This could be where you splash out – on a professional chef to oversee the reheating and cooking, and, vitally, the preparation. Make sure they have plenty of helpers and waiting staff at their disposal; anything less is a false economy.

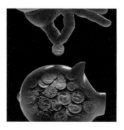  

Q **We've got to save wherever we can; we might even have to forget food at the wedding altogether. Is that acceptable?**

How did it go?

A *If that's the only way you can do it, it'll have to be. The best way to handle this is to hold your wedding late in the day, and invite your evening guests at a time that is obviously for dancing, not dining, such as seven-thirty or eight. You will have to consider the needs of your ceremony guests, though – how about stretching to some hearty canapés? Even if your wedding is at six, the guests will probably have been travelling and waiting in the pews for at least a couple of hours; they'll need some kind of sustenance.*

Q **What happens if we can't afford fancy ingredients, let alone a caterer?**

A *Then enlist some friends to make delicious, rustic doorstep sandwiches that you can pile up on huge plates. Place little flags in them to let everyone know what they are, and lay them out on checked table cloths. Make a style virtue of a hearty country offering. It certainly will be appreciated.*

36

Choosing a theme for decoration

This is much less frightening than you might think. You can take anything for inspiration – a favourite colour, a period from history, even your top film. Be careful, though, not to make your wedding seem like a budget trip to Disneyland.

Whatever theme you want for your wedding, you must research and create it properly. Don't try to go for a medieval look in your local village hall unless you do want it to seem like panto. However, if you have a local banqueting hall in a castle, then you'll have a good chance of pulling it off.

Flowers for the reception, like everything else, should fit your theme. This means more than just choosing blooms that are the right colour. A country themed

Choose your menu to reflect your theme if you are aiming for maximum effect. Winter formal dinners should offer some hearty, warming fare, ideally using seasonal ingredients. Mint and lemon are fresh flavours for spring weddings. Hot summer days call for light salads, berry sorbets and a classic summer drink, such as elderberry cordial. Consider your presentation. If you are planning a very minimal wedding, white platters in graphic shapes can be used to great effect with sushi. A casual affair in your parents' back garden by the sea could have aluminium buckets (new, of course!) with oysters in ice. Try adding little touches to drinks, such as borage flower heads (or other edible flowers) in your ice cubes so they clink prettily in summer cocktails. Just make sure to use mineral water so that the ice isn't cloudy, spoiling the effect.

wedding will lose its continuity if you plump for graphic, modern arrangements. Try using snowdrops or miniature daffodils planted in little buckets, or large headed, blowsy roses in old-fashioned colours such as dusky pinks and pale lemons. Think about the time of day: if you're having a winter reception, maybe in the evening, a rich, deep colour theme with lots of greenery will add to the drama of the event, whereas pale colours may get lost and are better suited to a sun-drenched marquee.

By choosing the right style and colour scheme, flowers can help transform a stark reception hall into a warm and inviting space. For an especially big space, you can rent small trees to lead into the room, or section off certain areas to create a more intimate feel. Lighting is also vital: make sure you avoid any stark overhead lights; if your room has them, ask if they can be dimmed. Tea lights on mirrors in the centre of the tables create interest and a sparkling focal point. Lanterns can also be used to great effect in marquees – try a mix of pretty pastel-coloured Chinese ones strung from poles.

SOMEWHERE OVER THE RAINBOW

Choosing a unifying colour, or combination of colours, is a great way to give your wedding a coherent theme and will make your efforts more noticeable. However, before you start, think about the bridesmaids. Your favourite colour may be yellow but you need to be careful with the shade – brunettes can look stunning in yellow but few blondes, bar Doris Day, can pull it off. So don't rush off and order hundreds of metres of yellow ribbon before you've thought about how twelve disgruntled maids and flower girls will look if their complexions are indistinguishable from their frocks.

Texture can be just as effective as colour. A seersucker gingham tablecloth with frayed edges is inexpensive to buy and easy to make, and will create a wonderful country feel in a marquee. Tie your table napkins with straw and a single oversized daisy.

Take a look at IDEA 11, *Coming up roses*, for more ideas on how to use flowers to their greatest effect.

Try another idea...

'I find that the harder I work, the more luck I seem to have.'
THOMAS JEFFERSON

Defining idea...

How did it go?

Q   We're holding our wedding and reception in the same venue, and the room looks too big. How can we handle it so we don't all rattle about in it like peas in a drum?

A   *You need to break the space up into more manageable portions. First, check with the venue staff if there's a way of dividing the room (this may be a situation they have had to accommodate before). If not, consider contacting a set-dressing or party organising company to come in with drapes and rigging to make a themed room within the room. Imagine the inside of a maharaja's tent – that's the kind of effect they can create, making the space more intimate and decadent.*

Q   Are there any steps we can take ourselves to cut a cavernous hall down to size so our theme shines through?

A   *Forget about using any top lighting (it will only show how high the ceilings are) and put candelabras on the tables. You can hire (from the catering and events companies that provide things like industrial ovens, chairs and tables) outsized black velvet curtains that have fairy lights embedded throughout them. Use them to divide the room into the desired space and create a walkway into your new, smaller environment. It will add a touch of excitement and feel very glamorous. Just remember to make the solution an improvement on the original rather than a desperate measure.*

37

Get me to the church on time

Want your wedding to run like a well-oiled military machine? Then you need some serious planning and a seamless ceremony schedule. There's more to organise than you might think, unless you want guests napping during yawning breaks and only fifteen minutes to do your hair.

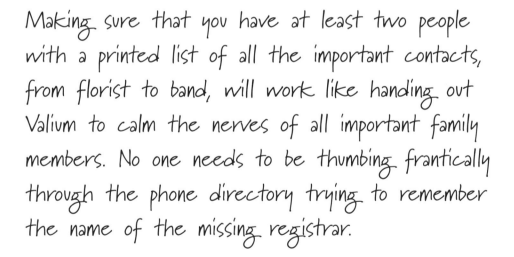

Making sure that you have at least two people with a printed list of all the important contacts, from florist to band, will work like handing out Valium to calm the nerves of all important family members. No one needs to be thumbing frantically through the phone directory trying to remember the name of the missing registrar.

Here's an idea for you...

With so much to consider, it's easy to forget those who cannot attend. Avoid offending anyone or causing confusion by sending announcements cards to any people not invited to the wedding because the number of guests must be limited, or because they live too far away. The cards may also be sent to other acquaintances who, while not being particularly close to the family, might still wish to know of the marriage. Rather than print them up separately, you could always make a more personal gesture by writing letters informing everyone of your plans and news.

ATTENTION TO DETAIL MAKES EVERYONE HAPPY

The best way to guarantee a happy day is to make everything crystal clear to everyone. Don't worry about looking like a control-freak – it's better than having to cope with chaos.

Consider a few extra little tweaks to make things run even more smoothly. Pew cards let special guests and family members know they are to be seated in the reserved section on either the bride's side or the groom's side. You can send them out with invitations and say they should be handed to the ushers on arrival. The ushers can be fully briefed to ensure guests smoothly end up where they should be, and that your stroppy aunt is treated with all due reverence.

Ceremony programmes are lovely keepsakes of the day. As well as spelling out the sequence of events during the ceremony, they also let everyone know when they are expected to be singing, sitting, listening or crying at the soppy bits. The ushers can hand them out (it's a nice way of greeting people and making them feel welcome) or they can be placed on the pews. Traditionally, they begin with the line 'order of service', and should include the bride and groom's names, the date, entrance music, hymns, prayers, marriage, benediction and any readings. You may also want to use the programmes as an opportunity to make any special announcements or thanks.

Take a look at IDEA 33, *And to your left...*, for tips on creating seating plans to ensure that all the guests are happy and chatty.

Try another idea...

SITTING COMFORTABLY

Seating or place cards let guests know where they should be seated during any formal meal. As well as avoiding an awkward scrum for the table nearest the buffet or bar, it gives you a unique opportunity to ensure that guests meet and mix. As people arrive, you can do one of two things. First, lay name cards out alphabetically by the entrance, and by number, colour or motif, guests should then be able to use the cards to find the corresponding table. Second, you can have a board that lists the names of each guest and shows which table they are supposed to be on. The guests should also have their places marked on the table with a name card. Have your ushers on hand to help any elderly party members find their seats. And bear in mind you may need high chairs and wheelchair access.

Defining idea...

Everyone has probably been to a wedding that's run over into mayhem – food nowhere in sight, then children crying and guests eating the table decorations (because they are so drunk on an empty stomach they no longer care). Your toastmaster, whether he is a professional or your best man, should ensure that events keep moving swiftly along in accordance with your planned schedule.

The reception should run in this order (or a close variation of it): the guests arrive at the venue and pass down the receiving line; the meal; the speeches and toasts; the cutting of the cake; the first dance; a big jolly party; the departure of the bride and groom; the departure of the guests. Hopefully.

In the final week before the big day, call all your suppliers and talk through final details. Make sure, for instance, that your florists know where your venues are and what time to arrive for set-up (they should know how long it takes), and that all of your suppliers will have adequate parking (you do not want your caterers circling the block for half an hour unable to unload the ovens because they don't have a resident's parking permit).

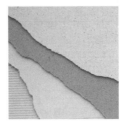

Q **I want to get married in my local church, but the only suitable venue for the reception is a good twenty miles away. Do you think that's a mistake?**

How did it go?

A *Not necessarily, but there are some obvious points to factor in. You should ensure that your ceremony does not end just as the rush hour starts and, ideally, you ought to avoid any trips that would take your convoy through the centre of a busy town.*

Q **Should we make a contingency plan for guests arriving at the reception venue who won't be going to the ceremony?**

A *Yes: make sure that should the worst happen, and you get stuck in traffic, someone will be on hand to greet them and start the festivities. This could be your caterer, who can have staff on hand to welcome guests with a glass of champagne while a harpist plays a gentle refrain. If this happens, you'll even get to make a second grand entrance.*

163

38

Twinkle toes...and other sparkly bits

As well as your dress, there are a few other vital weapons you need in your bridal outfit armoury. Looking effortlessly gorgeous takes a surprising amount of planning.

There is more to enhancing your radiance than the jewellery and other accessories on show. Without comfortable underwear and shoes as well, your beaming smile might crack into an expression of pain by the end of the day.

THE FUNDAMENTALS

The most important of all of your wedding accessories will be your 'scaffolding'. The underwear you choose has to operate on several levels – as well as beautiful, it needs to be comfortable and fit like a glove so no lines, lumps or bumps show under your gown.

Consider the season. Winter may call for gloves, a wrap or even a heavy (but still glamorous) coat. Summer might call for a light wrap or parasol against the sun. If you are having an outdoor reception, remember that when the sun goes down a chill may descend too. If you don't want a wrap or jacket, try a pretty cashmere cardigan in a '50s style. And if you are having an April wedding, don't forget umbrellas – or for a cute, quirky look buy your bridesmaids see-through macs to pop over their pretty frocks if the heavens open.

Your first step is to get yourself measured properly. It has been estimated that around 75 per cent of women in Britain wear the wrong size bra, so go to your local lingerie shop or department store and see a professional. And work out what time of your menstrual cycle you will be in on the day – a lot of women suffer water retention at certain times and can go up as much as a full cup size, which means your slinky lines could be more curvy than you banked on. You may also like the idea of surprising him with the full stockings and suspenders number, but if they are going to show under the dress try lace topped hold-ups instead.

When looking for underwear, remember that skin tone shades are much less likely to show through thin fabrics than white. French knickers can also give a smoother line than briefs or a G-string, so look at all styles, including the ones that you never wear. You'll need the right type of bra, too, especially if you have a strapless dress. It must give you support without digging in. Try on lots until you find the right style for your shape. Some dresses have built-in support, which may be worth considering. If you want to wear a figure-flattering undergarment that tucks in certain parts and flattens others, switch your sexy focus to nightwear instead so you can slope off after the reception and change into your own wedding present for him. That way you save flimsy for later and you won't have to go without support during the day.

SHOES

There are few women who don't relish the idea of a new pair of shoes, but this time there's a lot to take into consideration so look before you leap (in them). You'll be wearing them all day, and that's a long time if you aren't used to wearing heels (and even if you are), especially given that you won't get to sit down for long. You need to choose a pair that are high enough to be flattering, but not so high that you end up staggering from one side of the room to the other. You will also need to dance with them on, so that slinky pair might look great but do they also having staying power?

Take a look at IDEA 5, *The Blushing bride*, for inspiration on getting the right dress to match it all with.

Try another idea...

The best thing to do is find your most comfortable shoes and use them as a model; maybe they have an ankle strap and therefore feel more stable. Whatever you choose, you must make sure that you wear them for a few days to break them in – you don't want to end up with blisters. Make sure the bottoms of the shoes are a little scuffed so that you don't take a tumble during a rumba.

CHOOSING JEWELLERY

When choosing what to wear on your big day, you should first consider the neckline of your dress. A simple neckline can take both simple or very decorative jewellery. A choker is best on a long neck, which also suits a slim strand of pearls at the base of the throat. If you have a short neck, a diamond on a chain might look better, or choose to wear more eye-catching earrings instead. Make sure that all

'Beauty as we feel it is something indescribable; what it is or what it means can never be said.'
GEORGE SANTAYANA,
US philosopher

Defining idea...

167

your jewellery works together. You may find that your pearl tiara looks fussy with your gold choker, so try it all on for size. This is often a time that family members could want to step in with 'something old, something new' so if you are going to be presented with your grandmother's drop pearl earrings check they go with your diamante choker. You can always be cheeky and ask in advance if someone has any plans to surprise you.

How did
it go?

Q   I want a handbag to keep all my little necessaries in. Do you think it's unreasonable to ask my maid of honour to carry it?

A   *A compromise would be to share one, but if you definitely want your own then it's fine to ask (or rather, demand) – after all it is your day. Just make sure it is a pretty purse, not a huge sports bag: this is for touch-ups, not rebuilds. (Remember, your maid of honour will have emergency essentials such as tissues, powder, lip gloss or stick, mascara, eye make-up pads (in case you start sobbing), hair spray, and a spare pair of stockings in case you need them.)*

Q   What can I do if I just can't find the right shoes to go with my dress?

A   *Bear in mind that if you can find the right style but the right colour is eluding you, it's possible to have shoes dyed to match your dress perfectly.*

39

Choosing a morning suit

Grooms: think you're going to get off lightly? Wrong. Your suit will be the most keenly observed and scrutinised outfit you'll ever wear. Get the right one so you'll look like you belong on the catwalk rather than in the litter tray.

This should be the most expensive tackle you ever buy, so make sure that you don't skimp on the shirt and shoes. And please, please invest in new underwear and socks — you don't want a damper on your wedding night, do you?

It may go against everything you know, but this is a time to bring in a little help. In order of preference, you should choose as your adviser a gay male friend, a stylish woman friend or, finally, your mum. You can't see yourself properly from behind, and you might not be the best person to judge how the fabric goes with your skin tone.

Here's an idea for you... **Get looking for some footwear that's just right. As well as being stylish and a perfect match for your suit, your shoes need to be comfortable. Wear them at least two or three times beforehand to make sure you can get through the day in them. If they have smooth soles, you should consider cross hatching the bottoms so that you won't slide across marble floors as the cameras flash.**

BRING OUT YOUR INNER SUPERMODEL

Morning suits are a classic choice for a formal ceremony, black for winter and a lighter more fresh grey for summer weddings. You don't have to do cravats; you can dress it down slightly with a shirt and tie and leave out the top hats if they really make you feel as if you are in fancy dress. A morning suit creates a great sharp line if you feel you have a less than sharp figure. Shine, matt and texture can all be mixed to bring character to a suit, so consider that as a refined way of expressing individuality without going to extremes.

And a key question is how fashionable should you be? You might feel it would be great fun to look back at a wedding that seems incredibly evocative of an era, but then think of a rerun of *Top of the Pops* from the 1970s – hideous. So think of classic images that are both stylish and able to stand the test of time. Is it Prince Edward's grey herringbone and blue tie combination, or perhaps Clarke Gable's dinner jacket? Or maybe it's the Rat Pack cutting a dash through a Vegas landscape. (Just leave the violin case at home.) Then go hunt out your own equivalent.

You can create a bit of extra flash with special coloured lining or a sharp buttonhole. It is the groom's responsibility to provide the buttonholes, so make an effort to choose something with a bit of pizzazz. Your florist should be able to help you choose an arrangement that will reflect the bride's bouquet. Make sure that it works with your tie (and even your socks, to be super smooth).

Do make sure you talk to your best man about his suit. After all, he will be in a lot of the pictures so if he turns up in a suit he picked up in a charity shop the day before, he could be the cause of your first argument. Although your suit and his shouldn't have to match, they should both be the same colour – brown next to navy is not a complementary pairing. Obviously this is less of a problem if you are having a very casual wedding.

Suit's sorted; how about the rest of you? See IDEA 21, *Grooms grooming*, for the finishing touches.

Try another idea...

A STITCH IN TIME

If you have ever wanted your own bespoke suit, now is the one time in your life you can probably justify it but make sure you order in plenty of time. Firstly, you will need to find a reputable tailor: ask snappily dressed friends or colleagues for recommendations. Select a good grade of fabric that will wear well and feel fabulous. Go for the best that you can afford. Choose a style you want: three buttons or four, or a classic suit? You can be as fashionable as you like, but a classic style is the best investment. At this stage, your tailor will take all the required measurements. Now is the time to talk to him about the slightly less than perfect bits you would like to disguise. Tell him how you'd like your suit to fall on your shoulders, waist and shoes. The great thing about a bespoke suit is that you can have it cut to flatter your silhouette. Ask your tailor for all the tips that should work for your frame. You should also consider adding special touches, like a snazzy lining or special buttons. At the final fitting you should be very exacting and demand any little adjustments you feel are needed.

'*Just because I have rice on my clothes doesn't mean I've been to a wedding.*'
PHYLLIS DILLER

Defining idea...

171

How did it go?

Q   I can't cope with the pressure of choosing my own suit – my fiancée and her family are such style fascists. What can I do to make sure I don't get it wrong?

A   *Ask her to get a series of images from wedding magazines and clearly mark out what she likes.*

Q   I would have asked her to come along but she wants it to be a surprise. How can I get a clearer idea of what her expectations are?

A   *Ask her to go with you to the tailor's or stores you are thinking of using, and give you a 'definitely not' list. That way you can have some pretence of autonomy when you choose from the rest and you'll know she won't be disappointed.*

40

Hold a civil ceremony

Holding a civil ceremony is an ideal way of getting the type of wedding you want. Basically, you can have a small registry office marriage and then plan your own second ceremony, which can follow any form you like.

You have to hold the civil ceremony in legally recognised, permanently roofed premises, but you can hold your own blessing afterwards, with your guests and celebrant wherever you like. Let your imagination run riot.

This is a great chance to do something very unique and personal. Think laterally: you could choose anywhere, from an orchard to a little flotilla of boats. You could borrow chairs and make a happy grouping in your back garden, or still have a very formal affair with marquees and an orchestra. It is an ideal way of getting around the restrictions of where and how to marry. (And by 2006 the laws will be changing to include a wider range of locations.)

If you are having a second ceremony and your civil wedding is simply the 'legal' bit, then be flexible about your timings. Check out availabilities – a Tuesday morning might be an easy slot to get, and you can reserve all your energy and resources for planning your main event exactly when and how you want it.

The vows in a civil wedding tend to be short, although you can add your own readings and hymns. If you are opting for a second wedding ceremony, don't forget to get involved in writing your own vows because you can say whatever you want, however you want.

First stop for a civil ceremony, is the Superintendent Registrar of the district where you wish to marry. You can be married in church, a District Register Office, an army, navy or Air Force chapel, or any building approved by the local authority. For a marriage in the approved premises, you will need to make arrangements at the venue in question and give a formal notice of your marriage to the Superintendent Registrar. Do check with your reception venue if it has a licence for wedding ceremonies – it could simplify your day hugely.

PROPER DOCUMENTATION

Some rules apply to everyone. The minimum legal age for getting married is 16 years old. In England and Wales, the written consent of the parents or guardians is required for persons who have not reached 18 years old and have not been previously married. If either of the persons is below 18 a birth certificate must be produced. You or your partner must attend the register office for the area where you live and give notice of your marriage to the Superintendent Registrar. Each partner must have lived in that district for at least seven days prior to giving notice to the Superintendent Registrar. If you live in different districts then each one of you must give notice in your district. A form giving the couple's names and addresses, ages and location of the ceremony will have to be completed, together with a declaration that

Take a look at IDEA 17, *Where: choosing a location*, for ideas on choosing the right reception venue to follow your civil ceremony.

Try another idea…

there is no legal objection to the marriage. After the Superintendent Registrar has established that he can take notice of marriage, it is entered into a marriage notice book and a statutory form is displayed on a public notice board for fifteen days so that anyone who has any objection to your union can raise it.

A certificate of marriage will then be issued. If notice of marriage is given in two districts, then one should be collected by the couple, as it will have to be produced before the ceremony can go ahead. The certificate of marriage is valid for one year once notice of marriage has been given.

When you visit the Superintendent Registrar to make the formal arrangements you will need to produce certain documents. For example, if you have been married before, a decree absolute of divorce bearing the court's original stamp is needed, or, if your previous spouse has died, a death certificate. Other documents may also be required depending on the circumstances (e.g. the consent of parents to a marriage where one of the partners is under the age of 18 years old).

'*A good marriage is like a good trade: each thinks he got the better deal.*'
IVERN BALL

Defining idea…

How did it go?

Q I'm having a civil ceremony but am unsure about what to wear. Can I wear a wedding dress?

A   *It's your day – you can wear jeans or a bikini or a full 15 ft train. Lots of civil ceremony brides wear a traditional dress. There are a couple of things to consider though. You might want to wear something in which you can travel easily or stay warm in. If so, try a dress with added layers, like a wrap or coat, that you can lose when you get to the reception and start dancing. Think about a snazzy white suit: very Bianca Jagger. If you aren't wearing white, beware hats in case you end up looking like just another guest. Try a headdress with flowers or mini veil. Do carry flowers, even a subtle corsage on the wrist. Make sure you feel like a million dollars, whatever you wear – don't feel the need to play it down just because you may have chosen a registry office. If you are unsure how to get the mix to work for you, why not visit a personal shopper to help you?*

Q Can I change at the reception?

A   *You can, although it might be nice to enter in your wedding outfit so that your guests can see it, and then disappear to change and make a second entrance.*

41

Let's do it in a tent

It's a British tradition, in some way embodying that 'spirit of the Blitz' fortitude, that makes a country known for its rain and erratic weather decide to hold dearly cherished social events outdoors in a big tent. Nothing quite says 'English wedding' like a marquee.

It is basically a style choice to opt for a marquee. If you want all the trimmings, such as flooring and fancy light fittings, flowers, caterers and furniture hire, you can expect it to cost about the same as a hotel reception. However, if you borrowed chairs and tables and did your own catering and decoration, it could be a budget saviour.

When choosing a marquee your first consideration should be space, and you obviously need a garden or field big enough to accommodate it. They come in a

There will no doubt be a lot of traffic between the marquee and the bathroom. Look into hiring a portable toilet or an industrial-scale cleaner for the trail of mud on your parents' carpets.

variety of sizes and styles, but if you consider that you will need a marquee of roughly 14 by 20 metres for 125 guests having a formal, sit-down meal, that should give you an idea of which ones to start looking at. Go into the garden with a ball of red wool and mark out the size of marquee that you think you would need or like (the wool is red so you can see it in the grass, by the way). Then you need to talk to a marquee hire company about what can be done with the available space. Alternatively, you can tell them how many guests you would like and they can tell you what you will need – they will work out the size from the numbers, so you don't have to. If the tables and chairs will be moved to allow for dancing and the arrival of evening guests, check how many it can hold in that format before you send out invites. After all, you don't want disgruntled guests squeezed out into the cold because you had imagined them happily milling about in the sun.

Don't forget that if you are thinking of having a band, stage, dance floor or buffet tables, say so at the start, as these will need to be added into the equation. If you feel uncertain about your needs, ask for the hire company to make a visit to the site to help you plan. Marquees are usually erected two or three days before the wedding day, which means that if you want to do some of the decoration yourself, you can.

If you are having caterers, they can often be accommodated in a separate or adjoining marquee, or sometimes in the same marquee behind a divider. They will need discreet access in and out of the dining area, and running water and electricity for ovens and preparation. You might want to let them use the kitchen in your home to avoid extra cost but be realistic about the space required and be prepared for the mess.

IDEA 3, *The world and its mother*, can give you pointers on getting the numbers of guests right, so no one is left out in the cold.

Try another idea...

I'M NAKED!

When planning your budget, you need to consider that your marquee will literally be an empty tent and will need lots of styling to give it the atmosphere of a celebration. Sourcing the furniture and decorations is easy – the marquee company can help if you want it fuss-free, or there are many other events companies which can provide you with tables, chairs, lighting etc. Just make sure that all of it will work together – you marquee firm is unlikely to be interested if the lighting doesn't work if it's not their responsibility. Other hidden costs are heaters (in the winter), dance floors and flowers.

'*The more you praise and celebrate your life, the more there is in life to celebrate.*'
OPRAH WINFREY

Defining idea...

How did it go?

Q   I really want to have a classic English wedding in a marquee, but I am worried about the space. Are there ways to make the available area stretch further?

A   *If you have French windows, have the marquee joining directly to the house. This means the older guests can retreat inside to sit down and escape from the disco later on. It also means that you don't need to allow space for tables during the reception. Second, empty your garage for the caterers, so that they can use it for ovens, fridges and storage, saving you a bit more garden space. If it's big enough, they may even be able to work from there.*

Q   Our budget is pretty tight. What can we do to make cost savings?

A   *Costs go up as you have a bigger marquee and more guests. You can obviously therefore make savings by inviting fewer people. Anything you can do yourself will also save money. Get some willing friends to help with the decorations. You can also have long tables instead of round ones, in which case ask everyone if they could lend you trestle tables or wallpapering tables and use your own cloths to cover them. Instead of hiring china go for paper plates. A pretty marquee created cheaply but with some thought will be equally as charming as an expensive one decked out to the ceiling with chandeliers and gilt.*

42

Arguing

If you get through the wedding process without arguing it is likely that one of you is either dead or wearing earplugs. Emotions will always run high at times like this. You will have to deal with people and families who are sometimes far from perfect and all of whom have an opinion.

Is his mum interfering far too much for your liking? Before you explode, remember that she's been waiting to see her little boy get hitched since the day he was born, and she'll have imagined it (her way) several times. Everyone must learn to tread with caution.

MAKING IT A HAPPY TIME

People often say that weddings are blissfully happy occasions. The reality is that it can be a very exhausting, stressful and anxious time. It is often the case that happy-go-lucky, loving couples suddenly find themselves arguing, panicking and battling each other over the smallest issues. But by remembering a few tricks, you can get through the worst and still have a good time.

Here's an idea for you... **Stick a photograph of one of your happiest shared times on the fridge door with a note saying 'Why we're getting hitched'. Almost all couples wonder if it's all worth it in the run up to the day. If you've had a rough day and think the world is falling apart because you can't get the hot pink Rolls Royce you wanted, then you need to remember that it's not the point of the day – getting married is.**

Firstly, no matter how long you've been together, you will be dealing with issues that you have never worked on before. For a lot of couples, that often boils down to money. Both partners may work and manage their own cash, but they might not have had to deal with shared finances before. It can reveal a lot of unknown personality traits you might not have appreciated before, such as the fact they hide their bank statements in their sock drawer and never open them. Don't imagine these problems will go away. Use this as an opportunity to discuss how things will work in the future, and if you feel unsure get some professional advice, such as from a financial adviser, who can create a sensible impartial plan for you to follow.

STAYING FOCUSED

Always defend each other to your parents, or anyone else chipping in their opinions, over the big issues. Discuss anything that might cause problems. If your fiancé's mum is adding to the guest list until it looks like a modern-day version of the Domesday Book, talk it through before you tackle her about it. Although it might be tempting to earn some in-law points by sympathising with them on a one-to-one basis, you will only store up problems for later when it's used against you with your beloved. Agree on a policy together and stick to it, even if you have private reservations. And no matter how irresistible it is to sound off, be careful who you talk to. While you think you are just letting off steam, others may have longer memories.

SPLITTING UP AND GETTING BACK TOGETHER

IDEA 14, *How to say 'I don't' and 'you do'*, will show you how to get some extra help to save your nerves.

Try another idea...

At times like this you need to make sure that you plan enough time into your schedule to have some completely 'non-wedding' time. That means you should go to a film, have a country walk or just go out clubbing; whatever it was that you enjoyed doing before you decided to get hitched. That will put you back in touch with your real-life relationship. Make sure you don't talk about the wedding or arrangements at all, or you may find that after the wedding you've forgotten what you did before and have nothing else to talk about. (And remember, every bow and posy may be fascinating to you, but most people can only take so much wedding-speak. Be self-aware and don't turn into a 'big day' bore.)

This 'non-wedding' time should also work hand in hand with some time on your own. The reality is, no matter how much we would like to think that the battle of the sexes is over, weddings often illustrate that it's really just having an amnesty; the female partner is usually the one doing most of the planning and organising. If this is the case, then make sure that you have some quality time for you. Plan a regular facial or massage. Try to delegate tasks and find something you enjoy that is totally unrelated to the stress of planning – and make it more than just talking to your friend over a glass of wine (although you can do that too), as she may be a bridesmaid with whom you are also arguing about dresses. Exercise is a great stress reliever, as is dancing, painting or learning any other new skill.

'I'd like to have engraved inside every wedding ring, "be kind to one another" – this is the Golden Rule of marriage and secret of making love last through the years.'
RANDOLPH RAY

Defining idea...

How did it go?

Q **I really wanted to get married but suddenly everything seems to be falling apart. My partner won't get involved in any of the planning and seems to think it's all my responsibility. It doesn't bode well. Should I call it off?**

A *Almost every couple you meet will have a similar tale to tell. It often ends up with the bride being responsible for the majority of the planning, so the best way to avoid this is to play to your combined strengths. Write a list of all the chores and divide them up. Maybe your partner is great at finances, in which case he can be made to be responsible for paying deposits and managing the money. Rather than repeatedly having to ask for help, make sure he's got the list and understands what his chores are. Then leave him to it.*

Q **How can I make sure he does do the tasks on his part of the list?**

A *Make sure all the chores have a deadline, and that you both know them. Give yourself plenty of safety time so that if things aren't done you still have time to rescue things. Try not to chase him up until the deadline has arrived – if you harass him, he'll become resentful. If he really can't be relied upon to take some responsibility, you have one of two choices. You can accept it and ask friends for help instead, or call it off.*

43

The future is here...

So you got married and it was a wonderful day; you've even got the pictures to prove it. But what happens after you've found the last of the confetti and everyone has seen the video? Your life together begins in earnest, and it can be tough at first.

Lots of people find that they feel a bit flat after the wedding. It's a completely natural sensation after having been the focus of attention for months, sometimes even years. To go from being the golden couple to being just like everyone else can be a bit strange.

THE FALLOUT

As well as falling back to earth, you can also suffer from 'marriage movies'. Even people who have happily lived together for years suddenly find they are in conflict. This is often because they have conscious or unconscious ideas about how being married works, like a film playing somewhere in their heads of every marriage

Most people like to remember their wedding day and why they got married by celebrating their wedding anniversaries. Traditionally, certain materials are associated with particular years of marriage, the theory being that they will replace the wedding gifts as they wear out. Good spouses never forget an anniversary. So, here's a list of the transitional gifts. Add it to your diary so you'll have no excuse for forgetting...first, cotton; second, paper; third, leather or straw; fourth, silk or flowers; fifth, wood; sixth, iron or sugar; seventh, wool or copper; eighth, bronze; ninth, pottery; tenth, tin; eleventh, steel; twelfth, silk and fine linen; thirteenth, lace; fourteenth, ivory; fifteenth, crystal; twentieth, china; twenty-fifth, silver; thirtieth, pearl; thirty-fifth, coral; fortieth, ruby; forty-fifth, sapphire; fiftieth, golden; fifty-fifth, emerald; sixtieth, diamond; seventy-fifth, second diamond

model they have seen from Doris Day films to their own parents. Even if you think this isn't the case with you, you should talk through how you expect things to change. Most people find they have new expectations, as they wouldn't have chosen marriage if they didn't expect it to transform their situation in some way. It can be as simple as feeling more committed, in which case maybe you expect your partner to reorder their priorities.

Hopefully, you have discussed all the key issues before now, but, even so, you should have a good chat about your expectations. Are you going to keep your joint wedding account? How will you divide your assets as a married couple? (Lots of people have their own homes before they marry nowadays; will you put them in joint names?) Do you want children? Do you even have a time frame for having children and is it the same?

WAYS TO KEEP IT GOING

Everyone has their own ideas on how to keep love alive, but there are some techniques that most experts agree on. Make sure that you keep your own friends and pastimes so that you have new things to bring to the relationship; it may be tempting to spend all your time together but for most people that becomes more difficult as time goes on. Everyone needs to have somewhere to let off steam.

Many couples feel that avoiding arguments is a sign of success, for others a screaming match where anything goes can be an everyday occurrence. Both can be harmful in their own way, from storing up resentments to making spiteful accusations, but the main key for any couple is finding a way to express themselves, that both are comfortable with, when dealing with conflict. Part of being close means that you can say things to each other that you couldn't to other people, but this sometimes means that courtesy can slide – 'please', 'thank you' and 'can I make you a cup of tea?' will go a long way to keep you both feeling appreciated. And keep reminding yourselves that there's more to taking care of each other than just stopping the joint account from becoming overdrawn.

What else makes your relationship different to the others in your life? Your sex life. This can often suffer in the run up to the wedding as you have so much else going on and can often be too stressed or exhausted, but it is one of the key factors that makes your relationship special. Your honeymoon can be a great opportunity to reconnect on this level before you get back to your normal life.

IDEA 42, *Arguing*, helps you navigate the choppy waters of conflict before the big day. The same principles hold after you've got back from the honeymoon and your new life stretches ahead of you.

Try another idea...

'*A wedding anniversary is the celebration of love, trust, partnership, tolerance and tenacity. The order varies for any given year.*'
PAUL SWEENEY

Defining idea...

CHANGE – THE BIG CHALLENGE

Hopefully, you will spend the next 50 years in a state of bliss. A big part of this is allowing each other to change. Be realistic: the disco monster you married can't always be relied upon to get the party started when they've had little sleep thanks to your new baby. Don't tie people into the person they were at twenty, unless you can guarantee that you haven't changed a jot since you met; not even your underwear. (Which, in itself, could be grounds for divorce.)

How did it go?

Q   Sometimes I do worry that my partner and I might not change together. How can I help make that happen?

A   Make sure that you re-evaluate your situation regularly, and keep questioning how things are working. That's why anniversaries are so important.

Q   Aren't anniversaries just a chance to get some nice pressies and celebrate?

A   Only if you don't use them properly. Book a nice restaurant and have a good old chinwag. It might seem a bit contrived at first, but it is a good time to reflect and recall all the good (and slightly dodgy) things about marriage during the past year, to take stock of the relationship and check that you are still heading in the same direction.

44

The soundtrack to your life

Choosing the musical accompaniment to your wedding can be tricky, but if you get it right it can also unify your whole day *and* the congregation. You may love a bit of thrash metal when you're riding your Harley, but consider whether you'll want to dance to it when you're celebrating your twenty-fifth anniversary.

Spend plenty of time planning the music, and make sure you look beyond the boundaries of your normal tastes. Not everybody likes thrash metal! Your choice has to span generations and provide an atmosphere of good cheer. And make sure it is something that both of you really respond to.

PRACTICAL STUFF

Not sure where to start? There are lots of options, from string quartets, harpists, solo singers, jazz bands, and even a full choir. You will probably need ceremony music, reception music (as guests arrive), and band and/or a DJ.

Want to make sure that your first dance is memorable and super sleek? Book some dance lessons so that you can cut a dash. It will also give you a chance to relax together and escape the stressful bits of wedding work for a while, and have some fun.

First, when you visit the locations consider their size and acoustics. The hotel manager, vicar or marquee provider should be able to give you some direction about what you need in terms of size, power and also, importantly, space. Also think about your surroundings: a spring church wedding might call for a string quartet whereas a night-time winter wedding might better suit a classical pianist.

Plan your requirements carefully with your musicians; don't just expect them to turn up and play as the guests are being seated. Ask them for recommendations – they will have lots of experience and might have some great suggestions. Make sure they get plenty of breaks and have ample space in which to play.

MUSIC FOR THE CEREMONY

There is more music for the ceremony than you might imagine. Firstly, you have the prelude, what the guests will hear as they are seated and wait for the proceedings to begin. This can be played by your harpist, classical quartet, organist or even on CD. Next, you have the bit everyone knows – processional music plays as you and your wedding party make your grand entrance. The classic wedding march music is 'The Bridal March' by Wagner. Other popular choices are 'Arrival of the Queen of Sheeba', Handel, 'Grand March' from Verdi's *Aida*, Vivaldi's 'Spring' from *The Four Seasons*. As well as thinking of the arrival music, you need to think of the recessional music (the piece played as you depart) and how they work together.

Don't be frightened of doing something a little off the wall – this is a buoyant time, everyone is happy and about to go and celebrate, so something equally cheery and happy should be played here. There are also 'interludes' during the ceremony, such as the signing of the register, when you may want music playing. Bear in mind you might also want hymns here too. There is also something called a postlude, which is the musical backdrop played as the guests mill out after your departure for the reception. This can stop things from feeling 'flat' if the church is suddenly empty and silent after you leave.

Make sure the DJ gets your party going by checking out IDEA 52, *All night long*, and making sure you give him the best direction.

Try another idea...

RECEPTION REVELLING

When selecting a band for the reception, ask them to give you a recording of their music or tell you where you can see them live. Some bands will only do their own set – and not play requests – so you need to be certain they will suit the occasion. It is common practice to pay the balance of the band's fee on the night (having paid a deposit to secure the date). The best man should have the money with him and deal with this. Even if you have a band, it is also common to have a DJ as well. With a carefully thought out play-list, you'll have the music you want.

'Life is like music: it must be composed by ear, feeling, and instinct, not by rule.'
SAMUEL BUTLER

Defining idea...

THE FIRST DANCE

What should your first dance be? It may be the first song that you danced to, or your favourite snogging song. Whatever you choose, you should be able to dance to it. If you don't have an obvious contender, maybe opt for an old classic that you could have a waltz to, or the popular song you hear everywhere that summer and that will always remind you of your happy day.

How did it go?

Q **My future wife is as wonderful a woman as she is terrible a dancer. I know she's dreading the idea of the first dance. Can we just forget that part?**

A *You can do whatever you want, but it's a nice tradition that adds another special touch to the day. If you do decide to drop the dance you should get your toastmaster or DJ to let all the guests know that you want everyone to do the first dance as a joint effort. Make sure they're not waiting for you to take a twirl or you could have a very empty dance floor. But are you sure you can't persuade her?*

Q **She really has no sense of timing so what sort of dance could I suggest that might persuade her to try?**

A *You could always try a waltz. A few lessons should teach her at least what her feet are meant to do, and then you can clamp her close to your body and take the lead. You'll look all manly and protective while stopping her from knocking over tables.*

45

Religious ceremonies

For many couples a religious ceremony is a vital part of making their matrimonial pledges. It is an essential part of how they see their commitment not just to each other, but also as part of their wider faith. Such ceremonies can add an extra layer of formality, though, so check what it would mean for you.

To avoid disappointment, talk at length with your selected celebrant about restrictions. For example, some houses of worship have limitations on the music that can be played (such as Wagner), the timing of readings and minimum church attendance by the couple. There are also simple factors, such as whether or not you can use confetti — some allow only biodegradable, some none at all.

Here's an idea for you...

If you want to be spontaneous start investigating how you can get a 'special licence'. This requires that one of you has lived in the registration district for at least 15 days prior to giving notice at the registry office. This is a more expensive option but it then allows a marriage to take place after only one clear day of giving notice (excluding a Sunday, Christmas Day or Good Friday). Be ready to provide certain documents to show the Superintendent Registrar – these may include a passport or some other form of identification. If either of you is divorced, you will need to show the original decree absolute of your divorce.

Some rules apply to everyone getting married in the UK, regardless of their faith: the minimum legal age for marriage is sixteen years old; in England and Wales, the written consent of the parents or guardians is required for those under eighteen who have not previously been married; and if either of them is below eighteen, a birth certificate must be produced.

A religious ceremony takes place in a venue that has been formally registered by the Registrar General for marriages. Some insist that you attend 'marriage lessons' and services, so do check with your desired church right from the outset. The first step should be to speak to your minister, who will talk you through all of the requirements.

THE MAIN RELIGIOUS REQUIREMENTS

For Roman Catholic weddings you need to be baptised and confirmed, and you will also have to obtain a licence to marry. You must also be a regular attendee of the church or attend mass at least six weeks before the big day.

If you want to add some special personal touches to your ceremony, take a look at IDEA 6, *Getting readings right*, which outlines the ways you can use the readings to express yourselves more fully.

Try another idea...

Although Jewish weddings are usually held in a synagogue, they can also be held in other locations. Talk to your rabbi about your specific requirements. Remember that you cannot marry on the Sabbath.

For Church of England ceremonies, generally you or your spouse-to-be have to live in the parish but you can ask to make a request with some other specific church. You need to get the approval of the vicar, who can facilitate this in one of two ways. He can either add you to the parish electoral role and you can be considered a regular worshipper, or you can apply for a special licence. If he is able to marry you he will arrange for the banns to be read on three Sundays before the day of the ceremony or for a common licence to be issued. These have to be posted to allow anyone to raise oppositions to the union. The vicar can also register the marriage so you do not need to get a licence as well.

'All marriages are mixed marriages.'
CHANTAL SAPERSTEIN

Defining idea...

In the Church of Scotland, it is the celebrant that needs to be authorised, not the location, and there is no residency requirement, although you must still register at least 15 days before. Other religions in Scotland still have to meet with certain restrictions.

MIXED FAITH CEREMONIES

When mixed faiths are marrying, you need to find ways of bringing different aspects of your ceremonies together. One way of doing it is to get married in a civil service at a registry office and then create your own ceremony incorporating the most important aspects from both faiths. Alternatively, you can have your ceremony at one church, say a Catholic church, and ask a minister from a different religion to come and take part. The ceremony will be recognised as Catholic, however, and must be completed in full.

Q   **My partner is Catholic, but I'm not. What does that mean about us getting married in church?**

How did it go?

A   *You will probably need to have permission from the local bishop, and this can be arranged by your parish priest, who can also tell you how long it will take. (Leave plenty of time.) As a couple, you do have to make some commitments to the Church – you will both be expected to have wedding lessons on the Catholic idea of marriage, and your partner must promise to bring any children up as Catholics. (Don't fret if you can't promise this; it's your partner's responsibility as the Catholic parent.)*

Q   **Can my sister – who isn't a Catholic either – do a reading?**

A   *Yes, she can, and you can even include non-religious readings – just check with the priest before you cast any plans in stone.*

46

Seconds out

Second (or seventh) time around? Can you wear white? Do you have to invite ex-spouses? There are a few additional things to think about if this won't be your first time. Don't worry, though – with your experience and maturity, you'll breeze through them all.

Legally, there is no limit to the number of marriages you can enter into, providing you are free to do so (meaning that you are widowed or divorced and can produce an original death certificate or decree absolute with the original court seal). However, the options can be more limited if it's not your first wedding.

There are, of course, restrictions to the kind of marriages that you can have second (or more) time around. You may be prevented from having a religious ceremony, although you can have a blessing by your minister. Only some denominations will allow second marriages in church. Start by speaking to your local church or synagogue about the options.

Ushers, bridesmaids, flower girls, ring bearers, best men and pages are all great roles for the various family members you would like to honour. Make a list of those people and see if you can find ways for them all to take part in a special way. You can always ask family members to do readings or even host tables so that they are all given a sense of place and importance. Having soon-to-be-step-sisters as bridesmaids can be a great way for them to get to know one another without the focus being on them.

ALL CONCERNED

Getting hitched more than once is not unusual these days, and despite the fact that everyone will probably be very happy for you, you will most likely need to tread with caution. The first important task is to tell all closely interested parties, so you don't run the risk of them hearing it elsewhere. Children from previous marriages or relationships should be the first to hear, to ensure that they feel special – after all, this will be a new family in their lives. Regardless of your relationship with the ex-partners, they should know as quickly as possible too. Even if things are strained, it is not fair for your children to deal with the fallout of spreading the news. When you make your announcement to them, you should already have an idea of how the future will look – where you all will live, what effects it will have on the others' daily life, how you envisage the children's relationship working with their new step-parent. It is natural for them to have a mix of fear and excitement, so give them enough warning to get used to the idea; not just the week before the wedding!

GETTING YOUR GUEST LIST TOGETHER

Another major issue is deciding who gets invited. You may have a very close relationship with your former in-laws, and want them to be there; or your partner's children may really want their mum or dad present. The Americans have a tradition called the rehearsal dinner, which usually takes place the night before the event. You could hold your own version of this some time before the wedding to introduce all key parties to one another – they shouldn't all be meeting for the first time on the big day. This should calm any initial anxieties and, with luck, leave you free to concentrate on your arrangements. Make sure you allow for partners and friends to accompany and support those who might find things a bit awkward.

Worried about where to put everyone? IDEA 33, *And to your left…*, will help you understand how seating plans work.

Try another idea…

WHAT DO I LOOK LIKE?

Again, here you'll need a little sensitivity. Don't drone on to your partner about what your last do was like – this is meant to be a fresh start for all of you. A lot of couples will also be paying for their second weddings themselves, so that might have a big influence on style. However, there are no restrictions here. As far as wearing white goes, do whatever you prefer: there are few people who adhere to the original implication that it represents purity, even those getting married for the first time.

'You can make those promises with just as much passion the second time around. Such is the regenerative power of the human heart.'
MARION WINK, *O Magazine*, 2003

Defining idea…

Do, however, consider your environment. If you are having a civil wedding, make sure that you dress suitably, and differently from the first time around. A second wedding is a great opportunity to do something that radiates your personality and how the two of you see yourselves living in the future. A big white wedding might have seemed right in your twenties, but in your forties you will probably have changed a lot. Maybe you've become an aficionado of salsa dancing in recent years and fancy a garden barbeque with a dance-off and hay bales for seating.

How did it go?

Q   We're planning our honeymoon and I really want my kids to come along, but my partner wants me to leave them at home. Who's being unreasonable here?

A   *As your married life will be about being a family, you really should acknowledge your partner's desire to spend your honeymoon purely as a couple. This will give you a good grounding for heading home and hitting the realities of your new family life.*

Q   What if the kids are too small to be left with grandparents for a whole two weeks?

A   *There's no point in going away if you will spend all the time making long-distance phone calls and fretting. Why not try a compromise? Perhaps you could arrange a short break so you can enjoy some quality time together as a couple in the aftermath of the wedding and then do something with the children.*

47

Tied to a lamp-post in Germany

Stag and hen nights are increasingly more elaborate and expensive, so how do you choose the one that's right for you? Here's how to get them right – basically, photocopy this and give it to your maid of honour and best man.

Traditionally these evenings were for each of the couple to say goodbye to their old lives with their old friends. However, some couples nowadays do a joint weekend of stags and hens. Just make sure you head off in the right direction when you set the wheels in motion.

MONEY, MONEY, MONEY

It's not easy to get the balance right, but do think about everyone you would potentially like to include. You may want a week in Ibiza clubbing and getting nice

Here's an idea for you... **Plan a dress code to give a sense of occasion, even if you plan to stay in. A load of men playing poker in dinner jackets will boost your glamour factor, as will a pampered hen in a tiara and dressing gown.**

and brown, but is it affordable for everyone else? (Think time as well as money.) You also won't be able to expect your beloved great aunt Agnes to mix it up in a club all night on her walking frame. If you are sure you want to do something big, be prepared to accept gracefully if people can't come, and resist the temptation to apply emotional blackmail.

There are ways, however, to make the large-scale ideas more affordable, such as hiring a villa or country cottage, which can make a trip away seem much more affordable. When it comes to making the finances add up, your best man and chief bridesmaid should be charged with the organising.

GETTING THE RIGHT RIOT

Listen, best men and chief bridesmaids, your idea of the perfect stag/hen night might not be the same as your guest of honour's. The fact of the matter is that opposites attract, and that includes friends as well as lovers. So don't plan something that they will find offensive or dull. Most brides and grooms expect their good humour to be stretched, but don't go so far that you alienate them.

Think laterally when planning your do. Dragging a drunk and motley crew around the streets isn't the only option. For sports buffs, a trip to a match, the dogs or horseracing can all provide entertainment as well as the hospitality that your guests might be expecting. More active sports buffs should consider a round of golf or a

day on the dry ski slopes, kayaking or a spot of
surfing. For any novices, signing them up to a
surf or ski school for the day should cater for
their skills deficit and make sure they get
something out of it. Make sure you plan this in
advance so no one is left out. Those feeling
brave can even take it one step further and try
a spot of camping; just don't combine pitching your tent on a cliff and a lot of
booze. Alternatively, you can do something entirely regenerating, like a whole day
in a spa.

**Worried about what your role
should be? Take a look at IDEA
26, *The supporting cast*, to let
you know what is expected
from your role in the
proceedings.**

Try
another
idea...

Any kind of activity that people can do together and gives a focus is ideal.
Remember that you won't know everyone that your guest of honour does, so you
may have to unify a fairly disparate group, including non-drinkers and older
members of the party. Be sensitive when making plans. You can always start the
evening with a nice dinner, which moves onto more raucous entertainment, so that
people can
bale out at different stages when they've had
their fill.

HOW FAR IS TOO FAR?

Shaving bits, leaving someone stuck in another
country and buying them sex with strangers
are probably all going a bit too far.

*'Everything is funny as long
as it is happening to
Somebody Else.'*
WILL ROGERS, *Warning to Jokers:
lay off the prince*

Defining
idea...

PLANNING: A GUIDE FOR YOUR BEST MAN AND CHIEF BRIDESMAID

Ask the bride and groom what they want, but remember that you don't necessarily have to stick to it. It will give you an idea if they expect everyone to head off for a week in Bali or just pop along to the local pub. You will also get an idea if they want their parents invited (some do, you know), and if there are any people you should be inviting that you don't know about, such as long-lost school friends. Make sure you get all the contact details in one go so you don't have to worry about bugging them and letting things slip. Agree on a date too, as they may have something else planned. Let all the invitees know the date as soon as possible, even if you haven't confirmed the activities. Make sure it's *not* the night before if you have anything huge planned – no one will thank you for wedding photographs that look like the happy couple have been dug up.

You will need to think about transport, and making sure everyone gets about safely. If you are partying abroad, ask your hotel to help. And let everyone get an idea of cost beforehand. The guest of honour shouldn't pay for anything so the others need to chip in for their share. If you have an itinerary, copy it and give it to everyone in case you get lost. Have the requisite silly hats, plastic teeth and embarrassing outfits all ready before you take the first drink, or you may end up being lumbered with hundreds of penis shaped balloons in the kitchen drawer.

Q **I want to do a proper hen night the night before the wedding but I don't want to look like the bride of Dracula and stink like a chemistry set the next day. Any suggestions?**

How did it go?

A   *Stay in.*

Q **OK, if I stay in the night before, what can I do that'll make it up to my bridesmaids?**

A   *I said stay in, not go to bed. A great way to have your hen night the night before the wedding and look even buffer, rather than rougher, the following morning is to have a big pampering night in. Everyone gets a massage, facial or manicure, depending on how skilled you all are. Of course, you could always get a professional in – a masseuse or beautician that can make house calls to help with any tricky bits. Just don't let a drunk bridesmaid loose with some hair removal wax if she isn't too keen on the frock you've made her wear.*

48

Commitment ceremonies

Not everyone can, or wants to, make a religious or legal commitment. Instead you could have a commitment ceremony, which allows you to signify your love for each other in front of your nearest and dearest. It can be as moving and memorable as a regular wedding.

If you want guests to take your commitment ceremony seriously, you should select an officiant they can respect. Do not leave it just to your 'hilarious' best friend who can't resist limericks.

A religious celebrant, or some other person affiliated with a respected group, can get you started by giving you an example of typical ceremony wording from which to work. If you are religious and can't have a traditional wedding (such as a same sex marriage) you might have a sympathetic rabbi or vicar who is happy to come along and do a reading or take part in some other way. If not, you can have a friend or respected non-religious figure take the role of officiant.

Unfortunately, same sex weddings are not yet legal or recognised in many countries or religions, so a commitment ceremony is by far the best alternative. A same sex wedding does, however, bring up its own set of problems. Weddings, like all major life events, can bring up lots of feelings and issues for people, not all of them pleasant. Check with family members and friends that they are willing to acknowledge such a union. You may discover that they aren't comfortable taking part in such a major public ceremony, even though they seem to be happy with your relationship normally. If you encounter criticism, make sure you have other important but supportive figures in your life a phone call away, to remind you of how exciting it all really is.

SAYING 'I DO'

A commitment ceremony gives you a chance to write any kind of vows that you like. You can, of course, run it along the lines of a traditional ceremony to give it a sense of *gravitas*.

Start your ceremony by getting your celebrant to express your intentions. This will let everyone know what you believe your commitment means. As well as your vows to each other, consider including other traditional elements such as the exchanging of rings, having a friend or family member recite readings, and of course, the best bit, the kiss.

If you are opting not to make a legally binding commitment, you will not be protected by the rules of law (although common law rights can apply after a certain period of cohabiting). You may, therefore, want to make some other changes to your situation. Doing this is also a great way of starting a dialogue about what you will expect from each other, and your relationship, as a result of this ceremony.

Financially, you may want to open a joint account and change the names on your mortgage. If you want to protect your partner's future interests, you need to draw up wills to include each other, and make him or her the official recipient of any insurance policies. They will not automatically receive the benefits, regardless of your living situation. Make sure you are listed as the nearest of kin in passports and on medical records to protect your right to information in case something happens. Speak to a financial adviser or solicitor to clarify things. Your situation will be slightly different if you have children so you need to seek advice if you are concerned.

Want to plan a big do? IDEA 17, *Where: choosing a location*, will give you some ideas.

Try another idea...

HAVING IT ALL

Just because you haven't gone down the traditional route, it doesn't mean that you should miss out on the nice bits, such as fabulous outfits, big party, a wedding list and lots of flouncy bridesmaids.

When deciding what to wear, you can do exactly what you want, and follow tradition or do something completely different and have everyone in fairy wings and jeans. Make sure that your guests know what to expect, though – no one wants to turn up in an evening gown to a Hawaiian barbeque. Make sure that everybody know what to call you, too – will you still be 'partners' or are you two 'wives'?

'Intimacy is what makes a marriage, not a ceremony, not a piece of paper from the state.'
KATHLEEN NORRIS, writer

Defining idea...

Q **We want a commitment ceremony rather than a traditional wedding because we want a pagan union. Is it fair that we miss out on the perks other married couples get when they book their honeymoon?**

    A *Of course not, but you need to remember that hotels and airlines need to make sure that every couple claiming special treatment actually are wed, or they'd be handing out privileges and upgrades all over the shop, which is why they usually require the marriage certificate. You can try either booking a honeymoon package (you might have to explain the situation to your travel agent) or speaking to the airlines and hotels themselves. It will be up to their discretion, but you may be pleasantly surprised.*

    Q **Is there an easy way to ensure we don't miss out on the perks enjoyed by regular couples?**

    A *You could always avoid all the major hassles by holding your ceremony abroad. The specialist wedding departments of travel agents should be able to organise all the usual flowers, cake and dinners, but without the official legal bit. That way you are guaranteed the special treatment.*

49

Have a great wedding night

So much thought goes into the wedding day it's easy to forget the wedding night. After all, surely those things take care of themselves. In reality, you'd be shocked to discover how many wedding nights end in disaster, or, more accurately, a chaste lump in a hotel four-poster. Make sure yours doesn't.

So, what's the wedding night all about? Well, the key ingredients are privacy, intimacy and, of course, a little sweet lovin'…

The honeymoon, which starts with your wedding night, has its roots (or one of them) in the Norse word 'hjunottsmanathr', which relates to the time when a bride was kidnapped from a neighbouring village, and then was hidden by the future husband. Their location was unknown, and when her family gave up searching for her, they could return from 'hiding', which is what the word means. In Ireland, the 'month of honey' relates to the strong honey brew mead, which they drank at the wedding and was meant to promote fertility. These explanations sum up the sentiment. So how do you make it live up to the expectations?

Your libido can be depleted or suppressed by being overtired and stressed, both of which are likely to happen to you in the run up to the wedding. Schedule in some decent rest in the month before your wedding, to make sure you are relaxed, happy and ready to roll, rather than strung out and desperate to turn out the lights.

RECONNECTING

It is not uncommon for couples to have spent time apart as the wedding day approaches, with hen and stag nights and last-minute plans all taking their toll. Consequently, you can't expect just to launch yourself into a love fest the minute you close the hotel door behind you. Intimacy doesn't just reappear without some effort. Take some time to refocus your minds back onto each other. Have a glass of champagne and enjoy the view from your hotel window, or take a bath together.

ALL IN THE TIMING

Most weddings are lengthy affairs nowadays, so you need to be realistic about your stamina. Don't party till three in the morning and then expect the performance of the century, as you will simply be too tired. If you really want a special night on the romance front, then why not consider leaving early? Make a proper exit while the party is still in full swing, then create your own. A good way of putting the party behind you is to book a first-night hotel, away from the reception. It will remove the temptation to go back downstairs for one last dance, and stop the best man and ushers from filling the bed with sausage rolls. Make sure that the hotel knows it is your wedding night, and be clear about any special requirements you have. Give them an estimated time of arrival and ask them to get the room ready. Low lamp light instead of glaring overhead light, champagne chilling on ice and petals across the bed will all create a wonderfully seductive mood as you enter. Call the hotel, or ask one of your attendants to, on the morning of the wedding to make sure they don't forget.

If you want to feel your desirable best, take a look at IDEA 20, *The body beautiful*, for hints on making sure you are as buff as you can be.

Try another idea…

DRINKING TOO MUCH AND PUTTING ON YOUR GLAD RAGS

This is one of the classic enemies of seduction, be it your wedding night or standard Saturday night. You should try to pace yourself and have a glass of water for every second drink. If you can't bear the thought of keeping your hands off the bubbles on your special day, then ask your bartender to mix you up a champagne cocktail with fruit and ice to keep you hydrated and the alcohol content slightly lower.

Slinky underwear is also a vital seduction tool, but don't feel that you have to wear something uncomfortable all day just because you want to be a sex goddess. You may also need to choose something special to wear under your dress if it is clingy or low cut. So you can always be a bit of a '50s siren and buy a special negligee for the occasion, making an entrance from the bathroom when you've slithered into it. For men, usually anything clean and new will suffice.

'*If sex is such a natural phenomenon, how come there are so many books on how to?*'
BETTE MIDLER

Defining idea…

215

How did it go?

Q **I've been with my partner for ten years and I'm afraid our wedding night is just going to be like any other – a ready meal and TV! Even fancy underwear seems passé nowadays. What can I do to spice things up?**

A *Think about learning a little sexy dancing, such as stripping or a hot tango. You might think you'd be embarrassed, but that's exactly the point of the class, to make you feel differently about your body, build some confidence and help you see yourself in a different light. Try it. You might like it.*

Q **I'm worried that we'll be so emotionally drained that we won't be in the right mood for anything much on our wedding night. Any ideas on how we could get a fruity feel to the evening?**

A *You will have a powerful sense of relief, maybe loss, that it's all behind you but this is the chance for you to relax. While you're sipping champagne, why not get the mood right by playing some erotic games as you wind down? There are many saucy books out there that could get your imaginations going.*

50

Time lines

There are lots of ways to organise a wedding, and plenty of different types of weddings to organise. Here's a plan of attack for you, based on the average wedding in the UK.

In some faiths you may be expected to attend 'wedding lessons' (a series of meetings to discuss the expectations you have of marriage) and a Catholic marrying a non-Catholic will usually need special permission from the bishop, which may take a little time. These sorts of requirements need to be planned for well in advance.

A year to the day before the event, you will need to book your wedding and reception venues. You should also meet with your celebrant to talk about the type of ceremony you would like and whether there are any conditions you must fulfil. At this point, you should also start meeting caterers to ensure that you get them for the date that you want.

Here's an idea for you...

Finding it all too much to handle? Get a professional in to do the work for you. A wedding organiser can take the pressure off and manage all the chasing and arranging. If they are good, they'll do all this with a huge book of contacts containing all the best suppliers in the business. If you are doing the planning yourselves, make sure that both of you read these pages and get a clear idea of the work involved and when it needs to be done. Many wedding stress complaints come from partners who feel they are doing all the work themselves, so divide the responsibilities up early in the planning.

Around this time, you should also start creating your guest list, as should your partner and close family members, to give you a reasonable idea of the numbers to work with. It will also give you a good idea of budget expectations and help you make decisions about sit-down meals versus buffets.

At ten months, you should book your photographer and/or videographer, musicians and/or band, and order your wedding cake. Suppliers who can only be booked for one job a day need to be booked up first.

At eight months you can start the more fun bits, such as choosing your attendants, best man and ushers. You can then get them to help you decide on the tough stuff like wedding dress, suits and their outfits. Remember, it can take at least four months for a made-to-measure dress to be created, and even some off-the-peg dresses need to be ordered from abroad.

This is also a time when you need to start confirming things. You need to plan flowers, and order them with your florist if you want something complex or out of season. Take a look at honeymoon brochures, and investigate wedding lists. You will need to register before you send out your invitations.

At seven months, plan your ceremony and whether or not you will need musicians. Visit your stationer's and order your invites, cake boxes (if you intend to send them out), reception cards and place cards, and the printing of the order of ceremony. If you want special cars or transport, book them now. Make sure anyone doing a reading has the relevant pieces.

Want to get started on the planning? Have a look at IDEA 2, *When: date and time*, on choosing the right time of year to say 'I do'.

Try another idea...

At six months, we get another dose of fun stuff. You can plan your going away and honeymoon clothes, and any hired formal wear needs to be booked. You might also want to send out 'save the date' cards if you have a particularly popular weekend in summer planned for your nuptials.

At four months, you should tie up any outstanding bookings, such as the first-night hotel and confirming the DJ or band. You might also want to think about changing your passport, driving licence, insurance, doctor – all the things that you need to have your new married name on. This will give you plenty of time to make sure the name on your passport matches the one on your ticket. Check if you need any immunisations or visas for your honeymoon. Choose your wedding rings.

You should now be entering a more peaceful period, one that allows you to spend time working out seating plans and making up your gift list. It is customary to send out the invites at least six weeks before the wedding, but do it as soon as you feel comfortable – you can then start making a list of acceptances to finalise the catering arrangements. Don't forget to include your gift list cards.

'Marriage is that relationship between man and woman in which the independence is equal, the dependence mutual, and the obligation reciprocal.'
LOUIS K. ANSPACHER

Defining idea...

219

At two months to go, make sure you have any missing pieces of your outfit, such as shoes, underwear or jewellery. You should also be able to start confirming numbers with your caterer. Purchase attendants' gifts and make sure that you have them engraved straightaway if necessary.

In the final month, arrange a rehearsal, learn any readings or lines, make sure the rings are ready, enjoy your hen and stag nights and get your luggage ready to send to your first-night hotel. Give yourself a pampering treat to get into the spirit of celebration and excitement, and to ease the stress of it all. It's fun from here onwards.

How did it go?

Q   **I've just got a job abroad and so we've had to bring our wedding date forward by two months! Am I going to have to kiss my glam wedding goodbye?**

A   *Not necessarily. If you are now marrying in the less popular winter months, you may be able to get the church and reception room you originally wanted (allowing for Christmas parties of course). These are the hardest parts to rearrange. And there are often cancellations for various reasons (such as yours), so do bother to check.*

Q   **What's the best idea if we can't get the church on the right day?**

A   *Then have a quiet, legal civil wedding early in the week and find a grand venue for the day you wanted. Have a celebrant present so you can do your vows again, as you would like them.*

51

When things go wrong

Sometimes the best intentions in the world aren't enough, and things go wrong. Here's what to do if you think you've come to the end of the road.

Feelings of anxiety and tension before the wedding are often just a case of what is known as cold feet. It can be no big deal, as it simply shows that people are taking their commitment seriously. If you are really concerned, pre-marital counselling can help smooth things out, or you could try speaking to your minister. However, if it really is beyond repair, then the sensible thing to do is call off the wedding.

Here's an idea for you...

Don't be frightened: if you need help, ask for it. Your whole present and your planned future life have changed in a heartbeat, which no one can be expected to cope with on their own. A counsellor will be able to help you come to terms with the news, whether it was your decision or not.

BREAKING IT OFF

The place to start is to talk to your partner, although you may want to talk to a close family member or friend beforehand to help you choose the correct wording or gain confidence. You can expect the usual fallout of pain and recriminations, unless you are very lucky and it is a mutual decision. If you are the receiver of the bad news, make sure that you contact your nearest and dearest for support – do not let pride stop you from getting the help that you will need.

PRACTICAL CONSIDERATIONS

Ideally, the person calling off the wedding should deal with the practicalities, although there may be extenuating circumstances. If it is a mutual decision, divide the task. You must expect to lose your deposits on most, if not all, of your bookings (and it is unlikely that any kind of wedding insurance will cover this).

Depending on the stage of planning of the wedding, invites may have already gone out. This is one of the most difficult and emotional parts of cancelling a wedding. You can handle it formally by sending out a printed card announcing the cancellation, or deal with it through phone calls or emails. You may not want to explain why the wedding has been called off, in which case ask family or friends to deal with this and give them an official line.

You should always try to return gifts, although it is not always possible. At the very least, a thank you card should be sent. Gifts not yet delivered from your wedding list should be easy to cancel, but your list service may demand a fee for refunding payments – check their small print.

Find yourself overwhelmed by the wedding plans but unsure how to change your situation? Don't let things get on top of you: see IDEA 14, *How to say 'I don't' and 'you do'*, for pointers on getting help.

Try another idea...

LIGHTENING THE FINANCIAL BURDEN

It will be up to you to decide who has to carry the financial burden, and whether it is shared or not. Be careful that you are fair to people who have not hurt you, such as family members who have offered to pay for parts of the wedding. You can try to minimise the financial fallout from this situation by checking all of the cancellation policies. For some there could be a cut-off date after which you have to pay the full fee. At a stressed time like this it may be hard to pay attention to such details, but remember that it could save you from paying for the cancellation for years to come.

If you are having the wedding dress made, you might be able to pay for work done so far. Your shop will expect payment but they may be prepared to try to sell the dress on for you. You can also choose to give it to charity.

'When you make a mistake, don't look back at it long. Take the reason of the thing into your mind and then look forward. Mistakes are the lessons of wisdom. The past cannot be changed. The future is yet in your power.'
HUGH WHITE

Defining idea...

WHO GETS TO KEEP THE ENGAGEMENT RING?

As with deciding who has to make the phone calls, what happens to the ring is up for some debate. You may simply want to reclaim as much money as possible from the wedding costs and decide to sell it, or you may want to hold onto it as a keepsake. As a rule of thumb, the person calling off the wedding should be led by the wishes of the second party, all things being equal. However, the wedding may be called off due to unreasonable behaviour, in which case the rules change again. Once again, think of the other people involved – a family heirloom should be returned to the family it came from, regardless of why the wedding was cancelled. Let your conscience be your guide and do think carefully. After all, do you really want to keep a ring from a wedding that didn't happen?

Q   **Unfortunately, I decided to call off my wedding. After all of the stress of the planning and upset of cancelling it, I want to go away. The honeymoon destination is my dream ticket. Is it ethical for me to ask if I can take the trip?**

How did it go?

A   *You'd need to approach this with supreme caution, and expect some bitterness. If your ex-partner agrees, you need to cover the full cost of the trip yourself. You will also need to have his name changed on the tickets and this will probably cost you extra.*

Q   **What if he says no?**

A   *Accept gracefully and check if you can reclaim some of the costs from your travel insurance.*

52

All night long

There's a knack to throwing a party, and if you don't want everyone to end up in the kitchen – or in this case, the bar – you need to follow this guide to get (and keep) the party going.

Good parties don't come easy, and the more you plan the better chance you have of enjoying it yourself.

The first step is to have a designated party handler. If you have a schedule to stick to, you will want to be sure someone else is in charge of monitoring it, and you won't want to be trying to help the DJ find an extra plug for his amp. The best man is a good candidate. Unlike any other party you will ever throw, it shouldn't be your responsibility.

When planning the schedule, allow for the fact that not all guests will be arriving at the same time. You shouldn't expect guests to hit the dance floor immediately; they will want to arrive, mingle with friends and warm up into the party spirit gradually. If you want your evening guests to witness your first dance, make sure that you allow enough time for the stragglers to arrive. A good way to make sure that

Here's an idea for you... **Make a track list of the songs you would like to have played. Give it to the DJ in advance; it will ensure that you are not disappointed on the night when you discover the last record he bought was purchased in the year you were born. Make CD copies of these favourites, or ones that you feel are most evocative, and give them to guests as wedding favours.**

weddings keep moving along is to keep people informed, so get someone to act as toastmaster. They can welcome the evening guests, announce the running order for the celebrations and introduce the first dance.

Think about the length of your wedding and make sure that you cater properly, with enough nibbles and drinks for each phase. A dry wedding would equal a complete disaster in most people's eyes but ensure that among the alcohol you have a great mix of soft drinks that are a little more enticing than warm cola. You don't want people passing out from either boredom or alcohol poisoning.

Some people aren't comfortable with children being at a wedding reception, so think this through beforehand and decide on a policy. If they do come, make it clear that the parents must be responsible for their good behaviour. Watching little Joey slide across the dance floor, toppling bridesmaids as he goes, very quickly loses its charm and nobody will thank you for their broken ankle.

LIGHTING

This is one of the key factors when planning a good party. A room with naked light bulbs hanging grimly over the dance floor will certainly not guarantee any kind of swinging mood. What you need to make people feel ready to shake their funky stuff is a touch of low-level anonymity. Talk to your hotel or marquee hire company about the effect you want to create. You can have lanterns or candlelight on the tables, or something a bit more flashy if you want to create a '70s disco feel. Also talk to your DJ about any lighting he usually provides. He might be able to save you money, or you may want to stop him bringing his lights if they clash with your theme.

IDEA 25, *Drink and be merry*, will help you organise that other party essential – the bar.

Try another idea...

GET INTO THE GROOVE

Choosing the right music is essential for setting a great tone for dancing. You and your partner may have met in the flickering lights of a techno rave, but not everyone is going to thank you if you book the same DJ for old time's sake. You have many different age groups and tastes to consider, so give it some serious thought. You will want to see all your favourite family members and friends hitting the dance floor, so a range of styles from different eras is most appropriate.

Don't forget that some guests won't want to dance. You need to make sure there are places for them to sit and relax. Don't have the music too loud in the early part of the evening, as some guests will want to chat and catch up with arriving friends; they won't appreciate blaring music.

PIMP OUT THE USHERS

Ask your ushers to keep an eye out for ladies of all ages, from five to ninety-five, and see that they get a dance. It's a great way to make sure that they feel taken care of and included, and it gets people chatting and mixing.

'Dance is the hidden language of the soul.'
MARTHA GRAHAM, US modern dancer and choreographer

Defining idea...

229

Q **I want a proper DJ at my wedding that my friends will really enjoy but I don't want to alienate my older relatives. What can I do to keep everyone happy?**

A *One option is to have a separate marquee for dancing that leaves other guests free to stay chatting and mingling in the main marquee. That way people can come and go as they please.*

Q **What's an option if we haven't got enough space for a separate dance tent?**

A *You could have a live band earlier in the evening dedicated to old classics by the likes of Cole Porter and Ella Fitzgerald. That gives a chance to those who want to dance to something traditional and refined. Then you start the hardcore dancers off a little later after the relatives have had their turn around the floor.*

The end...

Or is it a new beginning?

We hope that the ideas in this book will have inspired you to go for your fantasy wedding.

So, why not let *us* know how you got on? What did it for you – what helped you get hitched without a hitch? Maybe you've got some tips of your own that you'd like to share. If you liked this book you may find we have more brilliant ideas for other areas that could help change your life for the better. You'll find us, and a host of other brilliant ideas, online at www.infideas.com.

If you prefer to write, then send your letters to:
Perfect weddings
The Infinite Ideas Company Ltd
36 St Giles, Oxford OX1 3LD, United Kingdom

We want to know what you think, because we're all working on making our lives better too. Give us your feedback and you could win a copy of another *52 Brilliant Ideas* book of your choice. Or maybe get a crack at writing your own.

Good luck. Be brilliant.

Offer one

CASH IN YOUR IDEAS

We hope you enjoy this book. We hope it inspires, amuses and educates you.
But we don't assume that you're a novice, or that this is the first book that you've
bought on the subject. You've got ideas of your own. Maybe our author has missed
an idea that you use successfully. If so, why not send it to info@infideas.com, and if
we like it we'll post it on our bulletin board. Better still, if your idea makes it into
print we'll send you £50 and you'll be fully credited so that everyone knows you've
had another Brilliant Idea.

Offer two

HOW COULD YOU REFUSE?

Amazing discounts on bulk quantities of Infinite Ideas books are available to
corporations, professional associations and other organizations.

For details call us on:
+44 (0)1865 514888
or e-mail: info@infideas.com

Where it's at...

Even more brilliant ideas...

Lose weight and stay slim

Eve Cameron

"Every week the media report on the latest fad diet that's sweeping Hollywood. Whether it's Atkins, food-combining or cabbage soup, there's always some new trend that promises to keep you slim. And yet at the same time we hear of an epidemic of obesity sweeping many parts of the world. It's pretty obvious that fad diets aren't working. "

"That's why I've written this book. There are countless tricks and techniques I've learnt over the years to help you become and stay slim. Losing weight successfully and permanently requires both a lifestyle and mindset change, and that's what Lose weight and stay slim offers you. Enjoy the new you!" – **Eve Cameron**

Available from all good bookshops and online at www.amazon.co.uk

Look gorgeous always

Linda Bird

"Looking beautiful is about much more than possessing fantastic cheek-bones and endless legs, though of course, great genes do help. The good news is that vitality, confidence, a savvy wardrobe, and a few great make up and grooming tricks can work wonders too."

"The trick is to look after yourself, and to learn how to use what you've got to your best advantage. It's about maximising your beautiful bits, minimising the less beautiful ones, and faking a few more. "

"Look gorgeous always will help you unlock the ravishing creature that lies within. It provides lots of simple but ingenious tips that I've learned from the leading lights in health and beauty. Try these brilliant ideas today – and feel more gorgeous, instantly!" – **Linda Bird**

Even more brilliant ideas...

Detox your finances

John Middleton

Do you know you're a millionaire?

"As an average citizen you'll probably spend at least one million pounds in the course of your working life. You're also likely to spend more than you earn, fail to realise your full earning potential and buy lots of stuff you don't really want or need. I know I did, but I decided to change. I had some ideas to get myself out of debt and financial denial and I put them into practice. Since then I've helped thousands of people sort out their own finances and now I can help you.

That's my story. This is yours. It starts here..." – **John Middleton**

Available from all good bookshops and online at www.amazon.co.uk

Create your dream home

Lizzie O'Prey

"You don't need a degree in fine art to make an outstanding home."

"Are you tired of those TV programmes that show you how to turn the living room of your semi into an 1880s French boudoir complete with louche lounging Casanova? And aren't you confused by the array of "the accompanying book of the series"? Which one should you buy? Homes are meant to be lived in, not gawped at, and people need creative but practical advice." – **Lizzie O'Prey**

238